I Love You
and
I Disagree
About LGBT

By
Donald Carter Rousu

To Ruth, my beloved wife, partner in ministry, partner in life.
May 26, 1967

"When God married you, he married a ministry."
– David Luth, August 1987

Introduction

1

Everyone Has Their Story

4

Early Success and a Heartache

21

Biblical Interpretation

31

The Strong Delusion

57

Born That Way

75

Gay is Not a Gender

89

The Scriptures

96

Marriage

106

Bibliography

Acknowledgments

About the Author

INTRODUCTION

Recently, a dear friend, Peter Fitch wrote a book that has caused me considerable concern. It is entitled *Learning to Interpret TOWARD LOVE, Actually Embracing People of Different Sexuality (in the kind of churches where they haven't been)* in which he endorses same sex marriage. Until a few short years ago, the church had unanimously agreed that the Sacred Scriptures unequivocally forbade such a thing. Now we have dissenting points of view, based on some new approaches to biblical interpretation.

When Peter's book was released, a mutual dear friend of ours, Larry Levy, wrote a letter to Peter, asking him to reconsider his position and the effect it would have on the Church. Peter, Larry, and I are all pastors in the same movement, the Vineyard Christian Fellowships of Canada. After having read Larry's excellent letter, I thought of writing one of my own. I thought I owed it to Peter and to the Vineyard movement around the world. My silence might imply agreement with his new position.

I had already discussed some of my concerns with Peter personally, and also with a few people in his church, prior to the release of the book. At the time, I did not know that the book was being written. Now that the book has been released and received wide circulation, I feel a need to publish a response that is equally public – a response not specifically to Peter, although he provided the impetus, but to the advocacy of same-sex marriage within the church, a position which shares a common body of repetitious rhetoric. Since the release of Peter's book, another Vineyard pastor-author from the US, Ken Wilson (no longer a Vineyard pastor), has published a similar book entitled *A Letter to My Congregation*. Now that it has come so close to home, I feel compelled to answer this rising voice. Thus, this book.

In all humility, I feel especially qualified to speak to this issue by God Himself. I know that may sound presumptuous, but all my life I have been praying with the Church, "Your Kingdom come, your will be done" and, like Madam Guyon, I believe that prayer is always being answered. I begin with the assumption that the totality of my life experience has been His will for me. I refer to my personal experience with sexual wounding from others and the consequent confusion it brought upon me, my theological education with a strong emphasis on biblical interpretation, and my thirty five years of experience as a sought-after pastoral counselor for homosexuals and mentor to other counselors. As the expression goes, "I could write a book." And if I am hearing the spirit of God aright, I must.

I deeply appreciate the title my friend Peter chose for his book, *Learning To Interpret TOWARD LOVE*. Beyond question, love is key. Love is essential. God is love! Fear and hatred within the church toward homosexuals is fully contrary to the spirit of Jesus, who requires us to love everyone without exception: Love the Lord, love your neighbor, love your friends, love one another, and love your enemies. This lack of love within certain sectors of the church, often highlighted on the evening news, certainly precludes the church from being an agent of healing or salvation in matters of sexual orientation. I burn with embarrassment and shame when the name of Jesus is associated with such blatant lovelessness and manifest rejection. No wonder that so much of the homosexual community perceives the church as enemy, not healer.

On the other hand, I am equally vexed by church leaders who, in the name of love, seek theological justification to embrace the gay agenda in the world and endorse same-sex marriage in the church.

I find it very hard to disagree with colleagues I love and respect so much. But disagree I must. Furthermore, I would prefer to disagree with my friends in private and defend their honor in public. But because my friend Peter and several others have taken this issue into a public forum, I reluctantly enter that public forum with them. I am confident that many will hear my heart, but I admit that I fear not being heard and understood by many others who have allowed themselves to become politically polarized and have already driven their stake in the ground.

Because so many in our society now worship at the altar of political correctness, I anticipate at least a few writing me off as hopelessly out of touch with the real world. Like most people, I want to be liked, admired, and accepted. I recognize that as the temptation to live in the fear of man rather than in the fear of God. Every time in the past when I have spoken out publically on this issue, there has been a price to pay. Those previous encounters were among relative strangers. They invited me in as a guest speaker because they had heard of our church's ministry to homosexuals. Most of the opposition was anonymous, cowardly, after the fact – distortions in the press, harassment through the mail system or over the phone. But that happened years ago, and our attention was turned to other things.

This feels different, because now I feel called to oppose, among many other voices, the writings of my own friends. It has taken me awhile to once again embrace the risk of being misunderstood, rejected, even hated. There are times that I wish Jesus had not said (Matthew 10:22), "You will be hated by all for my name's sake." I am acutely aware of the fact that this arena is one place where this is most likely to occur. So be it. It's time to take down the walls of sinful self-protection and appeal to the One who said to Abram, "I AM your shield; your reward shall be very great (Genesis 15:1)."

3

EVERYONE HAS THEIR STORY

After I read Peter's book, *Learning to Interpret TOWARD LOVE,* I put it down for a few days of rumination. By rumination, an image from livestock who chew their cud, I mean that I chose to not consciously think analytically and critically about the book, but rather to see what would rise back to the surface unbidden.

What came to the surface was Peter's personal story. What I knew even before I read the book is that Peter is a beloved professor in the academic community of St. Stephen's University (SSU) and has been for more than 30 years. At one point, Peter served as the acting president. SSU is a university that is known for two things: 1) It is very small (never more than 120 students) and has continued to survive financially only because of the extraordinary vision and sacrificial commitment of its faculty; and 2) It offers one of the best liberal arts programs on the planet because their classrooms are literally all over the world, with onsite education in Europe and Asia! They have pioneered a model that is being mimicked by others. See what I mean at http://ssu.ca

In the great arena of higher education, a university must promote itself on the basis of its vision and its admittance policies. St. Stephen's University began in 1975 as a trans-denominational ministry. People who wanted to know if it was "liberal" or "conservative" were frustrated to discover that SSU couldn't easily be pigeon-holed into those categories. Institutions that promote themselves in that way tend to teach their students what to think, rather than how to think. SSU clearly fosters the latter approach. Rather than promoting itself as either "liberal" or "conservative," SSU has sought to portray itself as a loving Christian community whose center is the Lord Jesus Christ.

Christian Universities tend to adopt rather strict policies for admitting new students, and those who are struggling with their sexual identity are generally excluded if that struggle becomes known. It is a political reality today that university-aged young people have become more accepting of a diversity of sexual expressions, and register some repulsion for institutions or authority figures who appear to be judgmental and closed-minded. I know that the faculty of SSU has struggled with this question of how they are perceived by potential students. How can a small Christian university avoid this intense polarization within our society, and simply be an environment that pursues healthy community under the Lordship of Jesus – that includes engaging with the issues of human sexuality?

Let me put it another way: The issues in our society around sexuality actually threaten the very existence of a small Christian university where clamouring voices demand that we join a camp and take up arms against the opposition. I know that these issues weigh heavily upon Peter and his academic colleagues, because he has spoken to me about them. And after reading his book, it became apparent to me that his experience at SSU has influenced his interpretation of Scripture. He has chosen the path, not of "liberal" non-think, nor of "conservative" non-think, but the path of love. I'm simply not convinced that the path he proposes is the same path defined by the One who is Love.

When I asked the question, "Why did Peter write what he wrote and come to the conclusions to which he came?" – that was the first thing that percolated to the surface: Peter's ubiquitous academic community and the young people who inhabit it. That, I believe, is a primary interpretive lens through which he sees. He not only shares their world with its shifting worldviews[1] but he has a genuine pastoral heart for them with their questions and pain.

The second major factor that came to my awareness was one I learned solely from reading Peter's book. I had never known that

Peter had an older brother who has been actively engaged in a same-sex relationship for a long time. I don't remember Peter ever speaking about it. In the same way that individuals go through the inner turmoil of "coming out" and revealing their same-sex attractions, so also the family members of that person have their own tensions about accepting these homosexual inclinations in a family member, and then telling others. One can be deeply torn between loving one's own flesh and loving one's God, especially when it appears that the God of the Bible demands we make a difficult, even costly choice. This tension can scream for resolution, and how long can a person carry this tension unresolved?

There is more, of course. Peter also says,

"Occasionally a student or church person would come out to me. I always tried to listen with understanding. I tried to communicate acceptance of each person without saying that I fully accepted his or her orientation. Sometimes I offered to pray for people, hoping, I guess, that God would miraculously enter the situation and 'heal' them. In one case, this seemed to happen (he recounts the situation) . . . But there were others. No matter how much listening took place, or how many prayers were said, no change took place in their orientation or outlook. I was mystified. Why didn't it work? If this was sin, why didn't it go away after it was confessed? If this was emotional brokenness, why wasn't it healed? I don't mean to be simplistic here. Real problems of any sort are not easily dealt with. However, the lack of demonstrable change in issues regarding orientation acted as a pearl in the oyster shell for me. It was an irritant in one way, but I think it was helpful in producing a better, perhaps beautiful, understanding over time."[2]

The fact that Peter talks about this factor as much as he does, and does so right out of the gate – tells me this has become a major influence in the way he now interprets scripture as it pertains to matters of homosexual relationships. I understand how that works. When there is dissonance between our understanding of scripture and the way life actually seems to work, we want to go back to scripture and ask, "Did I really hear the intent of scripture on this matter? Do I really have the heart of God? Or has the church traditionally read something into the scriptures that isn't really there? Is it time to re-consider our interpretation?" I say this with a heart of compassion, even though I think the resolution of that tension has led to a wrong conclusion.

I understand that, because I've travelled that road myself. The "conservative" Lutheran body in which I was raised, and in which I also pastored for 18 years, had an interpretation of the Scriptures which ruled out any present day manifestations of spiritual gifts. The party line was that such things ceased (thus, the term "cessationism" for that theological mindset) with the death of the last apostle. In my earliest years, I was so captured by that mindset that I could only see that point of view when I looked at the *proof texts* that had been cited by the theological experts of that day. But there were three things that moved me to reconsider: 1) The utter lack of any spiritual vitality in my own life, plus the hunger for what I lacked; 2) the general lack of spiritual vitality within the insular and cerebrally-oriented church that birthed and mothered me; and 3) the compelling testimonies of same-denomination friends who had seen, heard, and experienced for themselves the kind of phenomena which the New Testament regularly describes as the manifestations of the Kingdom of God. Specifically, they told me about speaking in tongues, words of knowledge, prophecy, and healing.

I flew back to the Scriptures and looked again at the *proof texts*. I found myself, time after time, saying "Wait a minute! That's not what that passage means at all!" This has happened for me over other issues as well, including the role of women in the leadership of the church.[3] So, not only have I spoken out on issues myself, but I understand Peter's desire to question traditional biblical interpretation on this issue of homosexuality, and to suggest that our interpretation in the past may not have been as loving as it ought to have been. But we'll come back to that later.

In recognizing the influence of Peter's life experience on his interpretation of Scripture, in all fairness, I must do the same with my own. The discipline of biblical interpretation clearly holds forth some common principles to which we are asked to adhere, but it would be foolish to deny the subjective element. We cannot help but interpret anything and everything through the grid of our own experience. I simply don't believe people who claim to be completely objective and unbiased. They deceive themselves.

I scarcely know where to begin telling my own story. Nor am I eager to tell all of it in a book. I have told it all, in finest detail, to individuals whom I trust with my life. But I will tell you, the reader, only those parts that help you to understand me, and my understanding of God's Word and will concerning the matters of sexual identity and sexual activity.

My story begins with the fact that I was conceived out-of-wedlock, in the heat of passion, by a man with an orphan spirit who needed a mother, and a pastor's daughter with a very sensitive conscience and a religious spirit. I know that such circumstances do not affect all children conceived out-of-wedlock the same way. But my existence was initially viewed as an *accident*, a *mistake,* the result of a *shameful sexual act* (fornication). I was an unwelcome surprise, and initially *unwanted.* My mother got over the *unwanted* part rather quickly, I suspect, but I'm not sure my dad did. Having been orphaned by the age of 11, he still needed mothering, not the responsibility of another mouth to feed. The point is, I was immersed in sexual shame from the start. I know that feeling all the way back to the beginning. And it colored the way I saw everything. The devil delights in such things to harass and oppress little ones.

In addition, all the evidence in my healing history points to the fact that I was sexually abused in my infancy, because my parents left me with an uncle who not only proved to be sexually perverse, but was jealous of my father. I was awakened sexually at a very early age. I don't remember any time in my life when I was not sexually aware and curious about sexual things. I know that a couple of adults around me took notice of that fact, and I felt shamed for it, so I began to try to push it away. I was mostly successful at repressing this sexual awareness and curiosity until I came into proximity with other young kids who seemed to have the same proclivity. It was a strange, non-verbal identification that I have now observed in adults who have similar histories of sexual brokenness.

For a kid like me, raised in a religious environment, sexual exploration and experimentation in childhood carried with it a secretiveness and shame that raised all kinds of doubts about my identity. I wondered if I was "different" from everyone else. In turn, those doubts made me vulnerable to the unhealthy influence of an older cousin who was sexually active. When I was ten years old, he taught me by demonstration some things about sex from his distorted perspective, then forced himself upon me. For a long time, I blocked it out of my mind as if it had never happened. He went into the military and I never saw him again. I had always admired him, and looked to him for his approval. The whole experience left me very confused, and guilt-ridden.

Although I was attracted to girls as a teen, there were a couple of guys that pursued me for "friendship" that involved sexual innuendos. I began to realize that some male friends wanted to have sex with me. One was in high school, and the next one was in junior college. I started asking myself, "Why me? Is there something about me that attracts men? Is there something wrong with me?" At the time, this was very bewildering and confusing to me, but many years later I gained some understanding about this from the writings of Leanne Payne, who asked the question, "Do you know why cannibals eat their victims? To gain their attributes, the things they believe themselves to lack." That insight would have been very valuable to me in my teens and early twenties! But unlike some people who are more vulnerable to confusion about their own sexual identity, I had a reasonably good sense of my masculinity being affirmed by my family of origin, most of my extended family, and my personal friends.

I was very active in athletics, particularly football and track, both in high school and junior college. It was in junior college that I began to realize that homosexuality and being effeminate were two different things. The quarterback on our junior college football team was exceptionally big, strong, agile, and masculine looking. Not only that, but he was an amazing athlete who had been on a full football scholarship at a state university prior to breaking his leg. I never imagined that he was actively homosexual. He began to take a liking to me, which I thought was great. While standing in line at the school cafeteria, he would rub my shoulders – which felt good. Then he started telling me how handsome I was. I thought, "That's a little unusual. What guy does that?" Then, after supper one night, he asked me to go for a walk with him. As we left the college campus, he started telling me how much fun it was to have sex with a man. Then he told me about all the men he had met at a big party in California who were into this amazing pleasure trip. He began naming a long list of professional entertainers who were there. I don't remember all the names, but I couldn't believe what he was telling me, and I forcefully said so: "B.S!" He insisted it was true. The one name that still sticks in my mind is Rock Hudson, who was the first of those he named to die of A.I.D.S. a few years later. After that, I was much more attentive to the nightly news. Often when a prominent singer or actor died of A.I.D.S., I would remember that he was on the list too.

I immediately told him that I wanted no part of his sexual adventure, and we returned to the campus. We continued to play football together, and occasionally eat a meal together in the dining hall at the same table, but he was no longer interested in me after I refused his advances. I'm not certain what became of him because he didn't return for a second year to that Christian college.

There is one more experience, this from my seminary years, that stands out in my mind. I had a friend who lived on the same floor of my dormitory, just down the hall from my private room. We spent many a weekend night in his room drinking good wine, talking about life, and listening to Bob Dylan. We were both in the same existential space at the time, two lonely unattached bachelors, and I called it "a theology of commiseration." My friend was a big, athletic guy with a very cool demeanor who was exceptionally self-confident and good-looking. He began to share a problem with me and ask for my advice. It concerned another friend of his, a classmate I knew but with whom I did not associate. His friend was an exceptionally bright student, a great actor, playwright, and director. He liked hanging out with the guy because he was interesting and had a fascinating personality. But lately, this fellow had begun to express his love for my friend and his desire to sleep together. He told me how this guy, over a period of weeks, was reduced to pleading, begging, weeping and crying. I could hardly believe what I was hearing. My friend said, "I don't want to hurt or reject him, but I don't want anything to do with his sexual obsession with me either. What should I do?"

We had so many conversations about this, for which I had no helpful advice, but I couldn't get it off my mind. I remember asking God, "Why are these guys like this? What happened to them? Why this lust for other men, this tormented craving?" Then I started remembering other people in this same state, in particular another cousin, a star athlete in University, who tried to seduce me one night as he shared my bed in our family home. In those days, parents didn't ask if visiting relatives could share your bed, they simply announced it!

During my second year of seminary, I struggled with a lot of discouragement and depression. I was tired of feeding my intellect while I was shrivelling in my spirit. I began to long for a gospel that made a tangible difference in the everyday lives of people. I was hungry for some spiritual reality. I literally began to challenge

God: "If I don't start seeing some supernatural things in my own life and ministry, I'm out of here! I quit!" And then I told him specifically what I meant. I had a prayer list of things that seemed to me to be in the category of "impossible." Near the top of my list was the healing of homosexuals and drug addicts. At that time, I would have considered such a healing a miracle. I was praying those prayers in the mid-1960s, prayers for various "impossible" conditions that were gradually answered, one by one many years later.

Now jump ahead a few years. I quote from a manual for healing that I am currently writing.[4] It seems important to share this story in both places:

In 1975, after nearly 7 years in ministry, my family and I moved from the United States to Canada. We assumed the pastorate of a church in renewal that began to grow quite significantly within the first couple of years of our tenure. Many of the new people coming to this church were single, young adults who were quite broken. It became abundantly clear to me that they needed healing. As my friend, Ken Dyck, author of *Freedom Session* says, "The harvest is plentiful; *it's also broken*." I wouldn't say they were highly neurotic or psychotic. In gentler terms, they were *dysfunctional*. By that, I mean that they could not successfully sustain human relationships with their peers, and were especially not able to function successfully in marriage and family relationships. And when they tried, they usually failed severely and quickly. Furthermore, most of them had no money to see psychologists or psychiatrists. I saw that if we as the church didn't offer the healing available in Christ, who would? Not only that, but I began to see that the church had a mandate from the Lord of the church himself in Matthew chapter 10, where Jesus said, "Preach that the kingdom of God is at hand, heal the sick, raise the dead, cleanse lepers and cast out demons." The church was under divine obligation to be a healing community! Would the church take this commission seriously or not?

I knew that if the number of broken people in our midst multiplied significantly, they would soon out-number the relatively-healthy ones and constitute the majority, and we would become a wholly dysfunctional body of believers.[5] Even though I didn't have the language for it then, I knew that "hurt people hurt people." And so we cried out for God to give us some kind of answer to our growing need for mental, emotional, and relational healing. God answers prayer! The first installment in his answer to our prayer came about six months after that first prayer.

An electrician friend whose wife had been healed of a deep depression spanning over several years introduced us to the writings of Dr. Charles Solomon of Grace Fellowship International and his Exchanged Life Seminar. All of this had to do with identifying the lies of rejection and appropriating one's true identity in Christ. It originally sprang from the revelatory teachings of Watchman Nee, then surfaced in other authors like Neil Anderson. We took the training and immediately began to see significant results with the people that came to us for counseling. But we had some counselees that were still stuck, and so we began to cry out to God again for more help.

Within months, the Lord led us into relationship with John and Paula Sandford of Elijah House Ministries. A pastor friend in our city invited John Sandford into his church to teach for a week and asked me if I would come and lead worship for the morning sessions. He also asked if I would serve as a technician for the conference to record all of the sessions and make those recordings available for sale. This obligated me to be present at every session and to pay rapt attention. God was in that! Within the first two hours of John's teaching on the first day, I knew this was the answer to our prayer for more help. We began to devour the Sandfords' books and audio lectures. For us, these two ministries of identity in Christ and the healing of the inner man fit together like hand in glove. And the healing results in our counselling practice seemed to increase exponentially. We soon gained a reputation as a healing church, and people came from far and wide to seek our help. We discovered an enormous hunger in the Body of Christ for counselling that was Christian in both content and spiritual power. In time, we found ourselves offering a course to train others who also wanted to meet this great need. Nearly five hundred people from multiple streams in the Body of Christ have taken the counselling course we first put together in 1991.

For whatever reason, a large percentage of those who began to seek my personal help were men who were suffering from acute sexual identity confusion, and some were very sexually active in homosexual encounters that were both promiscuous and anonymous. Although we lacked experience, we were full of faith that what God was teaching us through our mentors would be effective. To put it simply, it all made sense! Truth has a way of shining. We serve a God who heals the sick and raises the dead, and commissions us to do the same. Our earliest efforts were crowned with significant success. I heartily agree with Leanne Payne's opening words in her book, *Healing Homosexuality*, when she says,

"As a sexual neurosis, homosexuality is regarded as one of the most complex. As a condition for God to heal, it is (in spite of widespread belief to the contrary) remarkably simple."

Simple is not the same thing as easy. There are often hard battles to be fought. But simple means that anyone can do it, or more accurately, anyone can be a significant part of the team that does it. I do not speak as a solo player, but as a member of a healing community, because healing is, after all, a body ministry. The church, the Body of Christ, is a new creation healing community, a community of wounded healers. As Dr. Larry Crabb says so eloquently, "We were wounded in community, and we need to be healed in community." More people need to experience the church that way.

This experience of ministering to people with acute sexual identity confusion (and other forms of sexual brokenness)

continues to this day, and the Lord continues to crown our work with success. Looking back over these past 35 years of pastoral counselling with same sex attracted people has been extremely fulfilling. University students, housewives, husbands, musicians, artists, school teachers, pastors and priests, professors, athletes, and entertainers have been among the many we have counselled and prayed with. So many of these people became friends of our family, eating at our table, and our family eating at theirs. Some of them are still in our lives so we have opportunity to observe their continued flourishing in home and family, while others we have lost touch with. How many people are we talking about? We regularly shred our confidential counselling files, usually within two years after our last appointment, and we don't keep statistics, so I can't give a specific number. If I could have foreseen that I would be writing this book, I might have kept track!

In the earliest years (we began this kind of counselling in 1980), more people came and experienced healing from sexual identity confusion. As the social climate shifted, and people became more sceptical about the possibility or even the desirability of such healing, the traffic slowed significantly for a while. Recently, we have seen more people coming again, looking for freedom from same sex attraction as well as freedom from sexual addictions. If we could account for only one healing per year over the last thirty-five years, would that be an insignificant number? I am confident that in the first three years there were more than a dozen, because I have the clearest memories of those first exhilarating breakthroughs! Those are experiences you simply don't forget. Keep in mind that this ministry with same sex attracted people was done in the midst of a full-blown pastoral ministry of preaching, teaching, founding a Christian school, weddings, funerals, administration, multiple meetings and so on where counselling is just one segment of a very full schedule, and the counselling itself has been multi-faceted, not just focussed on sexual identity issues. However, of the hundreds of people we have counselled or led through healing programs, there are practically none that did not require and receive healing concerning sexual issues that impaired their ability to function happily in marriage or singleness. Acute sexual identity confusion needs to be seen within that larger context as just a part of a much bigger picture.

There are full-time counsellors and therapists who specialize in the field of sexuality who do publish statistics, and some of them claim hundreds of their clients have been re-oriented from same sex attraction to opposite sex attraction.[6] Without exaggeration, I can say that both my wife and I have seen *scores* of people in our own experience, both men and women, set free from acute sexual identity confusion, but how many does it take to convince us that it is even possible? If one man rose from the dead to never die again, we call that the first fruits of the resurrection of all the dead! One man! I understand that possibility and probability are not the same thing, but once we have established possibility, then we need to go on to probability. Is our faith bound to the probability statistics of social science, or some failed attempts by the inexperienced, or do we believe in the God who raises the dead?

Let me say clearly that ministering to people with acute sexual identity confusion does require some insight and training from those more experienced. I can't help but think of the story in the New Testament when the disciples of Jesus were asked to minister deliverance to a little boy, and they had no success, so they asked Jesus, "Why couldn't we cast it out?" In the Matthean account, He says, "Because of your little faith." In the Markan account, He says, "*This kind* cannot be driven out by anything but prayer and fasting (*emphasis mine*)."[7] Not everything is dealt with in the same way.

One of the things that perplexes me is the large number of people who say they want to do the kingdom ministry of Jesus, and yet are reluctant to spend the time and energy to get as well equipped as possible to do effective ministry. I feel so deeply indebted to the pioneers of the inner healing movement in the church who learned so much by fasting and prayer, trial and error, endured misunderstanding and rejection, wrote the books, and tirelessly taught any and all who would learn. I think in many ways they were the true prophets of the age, and many of them are passing on now. I don't feel worthy to stand in their company.

Part of the reason I chose to write this book is because of my humble and limited personal experience as a pastoral counselor. Like the apostles said in Acts 4:20, "We cannot stop telling about everything we have seen and heard (NLT)." Without arrogance, I have to say that I know what I know.

Of course, there are the detractors as well. One prominent ministry in years past for the healing of homosexuals, Exodus International, has now done an about-face, claiming that they have failed to accomplish such healing, *therefore* such healing is not possible, and apologizing to the gay community.[8] I personally have not been able to find out what therapeutic approach they employed, but I am well aware of approaches that are not effective. Their demise, of course, has added fuel to the fire for those who insist that change is not possible and "reparative therapy" or "conversion therapy" is abusive and needs to be banned. This position has become extremely political and people like US President Obama and presidential hopeful, Hillary Clinton, have taken up the cause to pass laws to that effect. Be assured that there is big money behind their bravado and a lot of political muscle. The environment for this kind of healing is becoming increasingly hostile, even to the point of censuring the kind of conversation we're having right now.

Nevertheless, I cannot deny what I know to be true. The prayers that I prayed so long ago for what seemed to be the impossible have been answered. Consequently, such things are now seen as fully possible. Experience begets faith and high expectation in the faithfulness and power of our loving heavenly Father.

I admit it. I am strongly biased by faith and personal experience. I believe in a Messiah who came to save, heal, and deliver all who call on His Name, and who commands and empowers us to do the same. I believe that the very reason the Son of God appeared was to destroy the works of the devil (I John 3:8), and that reason defines our mission. I believe that the primary function of the Church is to be a healing community, and we need to pursue our God-given destiny with all that we are and have.

Like I said, everyone has their story, and that's mine. This is my story, my perspective, and my interpretive lens. In the words of Henri Nouwen, I am a *wounded healer*. I knew my need, and I saw the need of others. For me, it was a deal breaker. I wouldn't have spent my life the way I did if He hadn't come through. But He did.

Does that mean we've never experienced disappointment or failure? Absolutely not. Not all stayed long enough to experience healing. Some came only one or twice to check us out. Some were pressured by their friends to stay in the gay community.

I remember one man, a male prostitute, who came to our office from off the street. We were in an industrial building at the time. He said he had heard about us from some friend that we might be able to help him. He said he wanted to be free but he was so stoned on drugs, I couldn't engage him on a meaningful level. I can still see him sitting there in his over-sized black leather jacket, short hair and gaunt face, staring at me with his expressionless face and empty eyes. He was so young and so utterly broken. I pleaded with him to get cleaned up a bit from the drugs and come back, but he never did.

We live in the eschatological tension of the Kingdom between the *already* and the *not yet*. Sometimes we get to see the Kingdom of God break through in dramatic ways, and other times, for whatever reason, we simply have to wait for the next opportunity to bring freedom and healing. But failure is only temporary, and a necessary step to growth in faith and endurance. Over the past 35 years, we've learned to do things better so that those coming after can profit from our mistakes.

Someone asked me, "But what about those who continue to struggle with same-sex attraction who neither feel 'healed' from their desires nor feel free in their conscience to pursue a monogamous same-sex relationship?" I have a number of responses to that question. Strong sexual desires are common to most people, regardless of their orientation, especially in the adolescent years, and our creator requires that we learn to restrain them and only release them at the proper time.

The essential insight of that is captured in Proverbs 16:32 (NLT):
"Better to be patient than powerful;
better to have self-control than to conquer a city."

Patience, delayed gratification, and self-control are so foreign to our instant self-gratifying culture that you have to know these values come from another world, a kingdom not of this world! In the same way that abstinence is the most effective antidote to teenage pregnancy and sexually transmitted diseases, so also abstinence from sexual activity outside of marriage is a path to spiritual growth and maturity.

In the course of my recent studies, I have been introduced to a group of Jesus followers who fit the description of same-sex attracted people who still experience those attractions, and yet have learned to embrace sexual purity (abstinence and celibacy) and lead fulfilling lives. They have an amazing website called *livingout.org* and they uniformly say that the key to joy and fulfilment is making Jesus the source and center of their identity, not their sexual attractions. They are all committed to living in continuous healthy community with other believers who support them in making daily healthy choices.

Some in our society view this as the church imposing cruel and unusual punishment on a persecuted minority, and imposing a burden too great to bear – as if having an orgasm is the highest good and an inalienable right of every man or woman. There, I said it. Someone had to! In a culture where medicating pain and pursuing pleasure is a universal value, we have a hard time believing that we can truly find deep and lasting joy and fulfilment in God and His family. I even know church-goers who don't believe that, and are still enslaved to all manner of addictions!

Having said all that, however, I have to say that in my own experience with same-sex attracted people, *if they persist* in the healing journey to the end – and it takes as long as it takes, sometimes weeks, sometimes months – *all* come to a place of significant healing from same-sex attraction or other destructive sexual compulsions. I know that many are sceptical of such claims, but it all has to do with a new identity, a fundamental shift in believing who and what I am because of my union with Jesus Christ. It is a revelation from heaven that changes *everything*! And in my ministry, I am committed to stay the course until everyone gets the revelation, the great AHA experience, and the lies are broken.

EARLY SUCCESS AND A HEARTACHE

There is nothing more heady than early success. Full of faith, I began to preach on the healing ministry of the church. I was encouraging people to increase their expectations and accept the invitation of God.

Before we ever began counselling in a formal way, my wife and I had already experienced much personal healing in our own lives. It didn't come through courses and textbooks. It came long and hard and slow through much suffering, biblical study, reading and prayer. When we finally got the textbooks and training, it only put structure and language to what we had already learned the hard way. It was particularly challenging for my wife. After she began reading the rich resources on Christian counselling, she felt a little angry and said to the Lord, "Why didn't you show me these things years ago? It would have saved me so much time and suffering." In essence, He told her, "I wanted you to be able to tell people you didn't learn about healing from a book. First, I needed to write it *on your heart* as a *deep inner knowing*."

When she was going through the darkest years of suffering on the way to healing, she was often afraid that she wouldn't make it, that she would lose her mind. The good thing is that desperation drove her deep into reading the Scriptures and spending hours in prayer each day. She often said that those were the only times when she felt relief from the mental and emotional torment. Sometimes, I too felt fear for her. She would frequently ask me to pray for her. There was a lot of trial and error on my part. Some things helped, some things didn't. It made me desperate for God. I needed strengthening and encouragement so that I could have some words of hope to impart to her.

Then the Lord shined His light on II Corinthians 1:3-4 and I spoke it over her:

"Blessed be the God and Father of our Lord Jesus Christ, the Father of mercies and the God of all comfort, who comforts us in all our affliction, so that we may be able to comfort those who are in any affliction, with the comfort with which we ourselves are comforted by God."

Full of clarity and faith, I said, "I know that God is going to use all of your mental and emotional pain to bless others. You will come through this victoriously! He is preparing you to have a healing ministry the likes of which you cannot presently imagine." And we both held onto that *rhema* word for years until it finally came to pass.

It was out of that crucible of suffering that faith for healing was born. And so I began to share that faith as I taught on Sunday mornings. And faith is a highly contagious thing. People began to call for appointments. I was not only eager to see people find healing; I was also eager to get as much experience as possible, because we already had an eye on the future. We were keen on equipping the saints to do the work of the ministry (Ephesians 4:12), and this also meant training other counsellors to join us and share the work.

One of the very first to contact me for counselling was a young man in his late twenties who was actively involved in a promiscuous homosexual lifestyle, and his self-identification was strongly homosexual. He had some effeminate mannerisms (not all homosexuals do) and wore the kind of flashy, colorful clothes that most men would never think of wearing in those days (this was 35 years ago!). Because he was a European immigrant, his accent also set him apart a bit. There were some in the church who were a little uncomfortable with his presence in our midst, but it was generally a loving bunch of people.

The Lord gave me real love and compassion for this young man, who had not experienced much love and affirmation from his own father. My willingness to fill that role was an important key to his healing. Central to his healing journey was the fact that he was experiencing the Lord's presence in our worship gatherings in a significant way. He never felt condemnation from the Lord, only gentle conviction. Although it seemed to him to be too much to hope for, he really wanted to be free from his homosexual compulsions and lifestyle. Another key factor for healing!

During the course of our sessions, we combed through his life history and identified areas of major wounding through the rejection and lies from parents, siblings, teachers, and peers that he had come to believe about himself. Then, with the help of some excellent teaching materials from the ministry of Dr. Charles R. Solomon, we sought to see and appropriate his true identity in Christ.[9] When he was able to see the truth about himself in Christ, the transformation became more and more evident. He was so excited, and so full of faith and joy at the freedom he was beginning to experience. Then we went back to his life's story and spoke forgiveness in prayer to all those who had sinned against him. That made it easier to take the next step, namely, to freely and deeply confess his own sinful reactions, and receive forgiveness. Each session brought more and more freedom, so that he wanted to make sure we didn't miss any dark or hidden things. The cleansing was deep and thorough.

Having dealt with the confession and forgiveness of sins, we then turned our attention to the *sin structures* that had been built up over time. I refer to false and negative conclusions about life and self. We began to renounce and bring to death on the cross bitter root judgments against self and others that lock and imprison us. We also identified and renounced bitter root inner vows that bind and keep us from a life of being led freely by the Spirit of the Lord. I am in the process of writing a handbook that describes this process in much greater detail and provides helpful tools to employ.[10]

When the counselling process was complete, he had let go of the homosexual identity and taken up his true heterosexual identity in Christ. He rapidly adopted spiritual disciplines that would help him to maintain his freedom and spiritual health. He eventually went on to be married and become a father, then got trained for ministry and has served as a chaplain for many years in an institutional setting.[11] Just a few months ago, I encountered this same man and his family after a funeral and in my presence, he told my son and his wife about the important part that Ruth and I had played in the transformation of his life. Then he said, "It has been almost 35 years that I've had this new life!"

As I said at the beginning, there is nothing more heady than early success. I was eager to get the word out. Not only had I seen the *impossible* happen, but I was the mid-wife! I got to watch the whole thing! It was like telling people that a dead person whom you all know has just been raised from the dead! But a wise counsellor cannot tell what happens in the confidentiality of the counselling office. Who would trust such a person?

So I prayed that somehow more people dealing with unwanted homosexual compulsions could find hope and freedom. It didn't take long for that prayer to be answered. This same fellow came to me within a few months after our weekly counselling sessions had ended, and said he wanted to share with others about his healing. He had been reading in the Psalms and was struck by a verse that said, "Let the redeemed of the Lord say so." He said, "I've been redeemed. I need to tell people." Furthermore, he wanted to know if he could give his testimony of healing on a Sunday morning in both the early and late services. We discussed it for quite awhile until both he and I knew what he would be saying. We decided that I would speak first to introduce the matter and express why we were doing this, then he would briefly tell his story, and I would comment at the end when he was finished.

That Sunday came and everything went off as planned. It was difficult at those services to gauge how the testimony of his healing was being received. In total, about 330 people heard him share. It appeared that all were respectfully quiet and attentive. By the end of the morning, I felt good about what had been shared, and I was grateful that the word for such a powerful healing had gone out. I was almost euphoric because God had been glorified.

The next day I got a call from this young man. He was crying. I asked him what was wrong. He said that on Sunday afternoon he received a couple of harrassing phone calls from two different men who had been at the service. They both called him a liar, and then hurled the same hateful epithets at him that he had heard all his life. He told me that he had gotten a new unlisted phone number, and he wanted me to have it. To this day, I have no idea who these men were. I was not only hurting for my friend, but I was angry – really angry that they would treat him in such an evil way! I was feeling such disappointment and despair over the church. I wondered how many more people, besides these two men, were unwilling to believe that this fellow was healed, and may be harboring fear and hatred toward him.

Now, about 35 years later, this kind of rejection of healing has taken on a strange new twist. It is not the so-called straights and homophobes who are casting the stones of skepticism and rejection, but those who are promoting the gay agenda and say that healing is impossible and even abusive! And so those who claim healing are still being marginalized by those who discount their experiences and stories of healing.

I began to see that the issue of homosexuality in the church was much bigger than I had thought. This wasn't just about individuals struggling with their sexual identity and finding help in the counselling office. It was also a corporate matter: Would the Body of Christ come to a place of faith and become a safe, healing community? Or would the church be the wounder, the rejecter, the tormentor? How would people ever find healing in the church from this and other maladies, generally viewed as *hopeless* and *unchangeable,* if the church itself had no faith, no hope, no love?

I spent a lot of time reflecting on that experience. I asked a few trusted friends what they thought of the testimony he had shared. Most were saying, "We'll give it some time. We'll see." They were trying to be open to me and my confidence in this healing, but they admitted to being a bit skeptical. So I kept pushing: "Why?" The answers were helpful. Some said, "He still dresses in those loud and flashy clothes." (Remember, this was 35 years ago in a conservative church!) Others said, "He's still effeminate in some of his mannerisms." I realized that external things are very big in the way we form opinions about others. As for myself, I had gotten to know his suffering and pain, and his deep desire to be free. I had learned to look past the outer things and the mannerisms in the sense that I was not put off by them. I saw and loved the inner man, and claimed him as my brother.

I shared with our newly healed friend some of the things I had learned from questioning church members. He was actually helped by the feedback. He told me that his unusual clothes and jewellery were very expensive, and it would take some time to replace them, but he wanted to take down any barriers between him and other believers! Whereas the clothes had been a statement of bitter defiance – "I dare you to accept me! You call me 'queer'. I'll show you queer!" – now he wanted to put away the symbols of queerness just as he had put away his bitterness. He eventually sold all of his expensive jewellery (He gave the proceeds to the church) and replaced his entire wardrobe. The mannerisms also changed over a period of time as he left the gay culture. He found a wonderful girlfriend, and got married. And by the way, he forgave those two men who called him after church the day he gave his testimony. He now knew that he needed to do that to stay free, just as Jesus did from the cross when he prayed, "Father, forgive them, for they know not what they do."

We eventually learned that his testimony had a salutary effect on two men in the church that day. Both were married but were secretly involved in sexual relationships with other men. Within months, both came for counselling and found healing from their sexual addictions, as well as from the fear and shame that come with them.

More and more men came to me because of their acute sexual identity confusion. Some had never given in to their same-sex attraction, but struggled daily with their mental and emotional compulsions. Others had multiple sexual partners, often with people whose names they either did not learn or could not remember.

Of course, more than half of the people I counselled in those early years came for reasons other than acute sexual identity confusion. Both I and my wife counseled people with chemical addictions, depression, relational dysfunction within families, destiny malaise, phobias, and so on. But something we began to realize that was common to nearly everyone's history was some kind of sexual brokenness. Addiction to pornography was common among men. An alarmingly high percentage of women had been molested or raped, often by close family members. Fornication was becoming increasingly common among teenagers and young adults. And the incidence of adultery was on the rise as well. As people went through the process of thoroughly forgiving others, renouncing bitter root judgments and inner vows, then making full confession of their own sins and making amends, we saw them come to life spiritually.[12] It then became apparent that sexual brokenness, with its consequent fear and shame, is one of the primary ways, if not the chief way, that the devil keeps would-be-disciples cowering in the shadows in hopeless defeat.

The light that exposes the works of darkness initially terrifies, but if we will endure its brightness, it soon brings peace and fellowship with God. The light changes and transforms us to the point where the apostle Paul says, " . . . at one time you were darkness, but now you are light in the Lord (Eph. 5:8)." How appropriate that he quotes this saying (probably from an early hymn) in verse 14:

"Awake, O sleeper,
   and arise from the dead,
   and Christ will shine on you."
   One of the greatest reasons for spiritual slumber in the church is sexual immorality (see the beginning of that section, Ephesians 5:3), and when we come out of that darkness into the light, it is like a resurrection from the dead!

Our ministry to sexually broken people eventually became known beyond our own congregation, and we were invited to speak about it in various venues. At one conference, I made a presentation to my fellow clergy on the healing of the homosexual. It didn't even dawn on me beforehand that any of my colleagues were functioning in homosexual activity. During the presentation, however, it became apparent that two of the pastors got quite agitated and wanted to argue, but restrained themselves. It seemed they were afraid of revealing too much about their personal lives. My hunch was confirmed when I found out later that both were quite active in the homosexual community, and they had come to fear and hate me. I felt perplexed because I had only been eager to offer hope, and stir the church to faith. I began to feel the opposition in my spirit. I also began to realize that this ministry could get costly.

Some time after that, my wife and I were invited to speak about the healing of the homosexual to the Alberta Federation of Women United for Families (AFWUF). We were sharing the platform with a former homosexual who had founded a parachurch ministry in the city for the healing of homosexuals. The meeting was held in a large downtown hotel. The presentation was well received, and there was an extensive question and answer period at the end. The next day, there was a lengthy report on the meeting in the Edmonton Journal. As I read the article, I realized that many of the things we had said were subtly twisted and distorted, often interpreted to say the exact opposite of what we had meant. I called the chairperson of AFWUF to ask about the article. She was very apologetic for the distortions and said that they had just discovered who wrote the article. A reporter from the Edmonton Journal, who I later learned identified himself as gay, had entered the meeting hall without registering and without their knowledge, avoided interaction with the delegates, took some notes, and left. Because his name was on the article, I called his editor and asked to speak to him. I was told he would get right back to me. When I didn't hear from him after a couple of days, I called the editor back. He told me that the journalist had suddenly resigned and left the city with no way to contact him. I asked the editor for a retraction, or a chance to respond to the article, but he said he was too busy for that and he couldn't very well do that in the absence of the writer. I felt frustrated at what appeared to be a willful misrepresentation.

A week later, an article was published in the Gateway, the official student newspaper of the University of Alberta. It appeared in the column entitled "One In Ten." It was a critique of the article about the AFWUF meeting that had appeared in the Edmonton Journal. It was obvious that this student writer had assumed the Journal article was factually accurate in every respect. Shortly after the release of the Gateway article, we started getting phone calls, most of which were abusive and obscene. There was a notable exception. One young man who called was fairly polite, and when I interrupted him and asked if I could tell my side, he deferred to me. After I spoke to the distortions and told him what we had actually said at the meeting, and what our ministry was actually about, he said, "Thank you. I really appreciate what you have to say, and I've changed my mind about you. You sound like a good person, and I feel heard and respected by you. I'm not sure I agree with you, but it has given me a lot to think about." Our parting was warm and cordial.

But that wasn't the end of the fallout from those two articles. For several weeks we were systematically harassed, and it was impossible to know if it was one over-active individual or a coordinated group of individuals. We began getting expensive magazines delivered to our house, and then we would get the bills for these magazines. Someone, or some group, had subscribed to these magazines in our name. I spent hours typing letters to the publishers telling them that we wanted to cancel these subscriptions which had been made in our name without our knowledge or consent. We were coming to a new level of awareness of the warfare over this issue of homosexual healing, something I thought was nothing but wonderful news.

Around that same time, a now extinct magazine called *Alberta Report* was attempting to present a balanced and respectful discussion of homosexuality. They experienced a very strong backlash from the gay community to that series, and Link Byfield shared this in a couple of editorials. He reported that they had received parcels in the mail containing used condoms and feces. I remember thinking, "Who would do something so disgusting? I certainly hope that doesn't happen to us." But it did. I would be lying if I said we didn't find that intimidating. And of course, those are the tactics of warfare. Like John Eldredge says in his book, *Waking The Dead,* "We are at war . . . you were born into a world at war, and you will live all your days in the midst of a great battle, involving all the forces of heaven and hell and played out here on earth."[13]

BIBLICAL INTERPRETATION

It is not my intention to give an exhaustive treatment of all the biblical material surrounding this issue. That has already been done to my complete satisfaction in a document that I had a hand in critiquing through an international web-based forum with Dr. Derek Morphew over a period of months. It appears in the bibliography as "Vineyard USA Executive Team on behalf of Vineyard USA. *Pastoring LGBT Persons,* Position Paper, 2014." There are, however, a few issues on which I wish to focus.

The title of Peter's book, *Learning to Interpret TOWARD LOVE,* tells me that his primary purpose is to deal with the issue of biblical interpretation, which theologians call *hermeneutics.* Primarily because of the philosophical influence of post-modernism, which has relativism at its core (what is true for you may not be true for me, and there is no absolute truth), the theological discipline of hermeneutics has been caught in a popular philosophical tornado where nearly everything is up in the air. I think it would be fair to say that post-modernism tends to attract those who deny the existence and/or the authority of God, and therefore the authority of anything that purports to be the *Word* of God. I also think it is fair to say that post-moderns in general question authority and "controlling narratives." This presents a problem when declaring the scriptural narrative as normative.

A quick search on the internet will reveal that most Christian denominations all along the conservative to liberal spectrum declare "that the Sacred Scriptures of the Old and New Testaments are the sole rule and norm for faith and life." That's what most of us Christians have said for centuries, but is it still true? Or have we come to the same state of affairs revealed so poignantly in the last verse of the book of Judges (21:25)? "In those days, there was no king in Israel. Everyone did what was right in his own eyes." The point is this: Relativism can and does have a profound effect on the way we interpret the scriptures. There are a number of new books on the market today that all ask the question, "How can we relate the gospel to a post-modern society?" I think a better question is, "How do we relate the *Law and the Gospel* to a post-modern society?" Am I wrong to say that the gospel is only for those who need a gospel, and know their need? I understand that the function of the Law (Rom. 3:20) is to show our need. It reveals what is out of order with the divine intention in God's orderly universe.

Hermeneutics is all about meaning. It asks two questions of the scripture: 1) As nearly as we can determine, what did this mean to the author and readers two or three thousand years ago when it was written? and 2) What does it mean today? How can we extract the precious essence, the Word of the Lord, from an unfamiliar culture across thousands of miles and thousands of years of time and transplant that powerful, life-giving Word into the soil of our hearts today?

We really have no business telling people what the Scriptures mean today if we don't know what it meant to them then. For example, the only commandment with a promise stated that honouring father and mother would result in living a long time *in the land*. Without a thorough understanding of God's covenant with Israel, we will focus on the promise of long life for every individual who honours father and mother. But that was not the ancient meaning. The focus was on the *land,* the promised land of Canaan, as the *covenant inheritance,* not on long life. Furthermore, the promise of long life in the land is not individualistic, but corporate. In other words, it applies first of all to Israel as a nation. If the nation of Israel would uphold this principle of honouring parental authority throughout their society as a way of honouring God, the author of all life, then the nation as a corporate entity would continue to enjoy for a long time *the land* that God promised to their father, Abraham. This explains the rather harsh treatment of children who cursed or physically assaulted their parents, or defiled their marriage bed. Death by stoning.[14] The inheritance of the whole nation was at stake! And one errant child could not be allowed to jeopardize the entire nation's inheritance. Our society today is so focussed on the "rights" of individuals, or the "rights" of minority groups, or the "rights" of children, that we have a hard time seeing the bigger picture and taking home the spirit of that ancient command that expresses the will of our creator. But, as scriptural history testifies, the people rejected the authority of God and His authorized representatives (especially the prophets). Consequently, the whole nation of Israel was driven *from the land* into exile, the ten northern tribes to Assyria and the two southern tribes to Babylon. They did not live a long time in the land. There are deep and painful consequences in dishonouring those who hold what Martin Luther called the *hidden majesty* of God.[15]

Can we see a parallel dynamic in the New Testament? In I Corinthians 6:9 ff., Wrongdoers (Greek: *adikoi* – those *out of line with* the will of God) are warned that if they continue to practice their acts of rebellion and immorality, they will not inherit the Kingdom of God. We are no longer looking at losing the enjoyment of a piece of physical land, but losing the experience of a heavenly Kingdom, God's rule and reign under which the blind see, the lame walk, the deaf hear, and the poor keep hearing good news. It also appears to me that when sexual immorality becomes known in the church (see I Cor. 5 in its entirety), it is incumbent upon the church, the community of believers, to bring correction and training. And if the church fails to do this, it loses its ability to become an instrument of salvation.[16]

I see so many wishing that God would seem real to them, but the experience of His presence and power has eluded them, and they don't know why. They haven't been able to see or enter into what the Bible calls the kingdom of God. However, if they heed His invitation, and deal with these divine authority issues that are attached to mother wounds and father wounds, they begin to enter into the inheritance of the promised Kingdom. So much of our prayer ministry is focussed on mother and father issues because it results in so much deep and lasting healing.[17] Malachi 4:5 & 6 has been key to this understanding:

"Behold, I will send you the prophet Elijah before the great and terrible day of the LORD comes. And He will turn the hearts of fathers to their children, and the hearts of children to their fathers, lest I come and smite the land with a curse (RSV)."

I cited the commandment about honouring fathers and mothers as an example of a Law that is universal in its import, sort of like the law of gravity, that always works the same way for everyone. It is given for our good. The ancient command has consistent and predictable consequences for those who either defy it or obey it. If I should chose to obey that Law, I will reap the promised blessing. If I should chose to defy it, I will reap the bitter consequences, *unless* I allow Jesus to reap them on my behalf. Here comes the gospel, the good news to all who have fallen short. As Paul says to the Galatians, "Christ redeemed us from the curse of the law by becoming a curse for us – for it is written, 'Cursed is everyone who is hanged on a tree' – so that in Christ Jesus the blessing of Abraham might come to the Gentiles, so that we might receive the promised Spirit through faith (3:13, 14)."

I raise this issue about the law because our view of the Law has everything to do with how we view and interpret the Scriptures. There is a great danger, in our zeal to preach the good news of Jesus Christ and his mercy, that we pit the gospel against the Law, and imply that the Law doesn't apply to us anymore because "we now live under grace." I understand this from a personal point of view. Living in the tension between the Law of God and the good news of salvation through faith in Jesus Christ can be almost unbearable, especially for a young preacher (I was one of those – a long time ago, but I still remember!). There is a term for those who try to resolve this tension by saying, essentially, that the Law has been abolished, something I myself tried to do for a period of time. Out of my zeal to avoid legalism, I became an antinomian (anti = against; *nomos* is the Greek word for law). But I couldn't get away from the counsel of Jesus Himself who said in the Sermon on the Mount, "Think not that I have come to abolish the Law or the Prophets; I have not come to abolish them but to fulfill them (Matthew 5:17)."

In the debate over homosexual activity, I hear some saying that we now live under grace, and that if we really love people like God does, we will approve and condone what the law forbids, providing that the same-sex partners are faithful, monogamous, loving and caring individuals.

That, I believe, is a form of antinomianism. But notice that it is riddled with conflicting choices. We either have to pit a loving God against his own Law, or re-interpret the Law: God used to mean that, but He doesn't anymore (which is a possibility between the old covenant and the new covenant *when He explicitly says so*); or, that was man's law, not God's Law (well, did Moses function independently from God?); or we make up our own law that says, "As long as same-sex partners are faithful, monogamous, loving and caring, they meet our ecclesiastical approval and escape censure." It appears that this last possibility is where the advocates for same-sex marriage within the evangelical world think we should land.

Not only did I have problems as an antinomian with Jesus saying,
   "Do not think that I have come to abolish the Law or the Prophets; I have not come to abolish them but to fulfill them. For truly, I say to you, until heaven and earth pass away, not an iota, not a dot, will pass from the Law until all is accomplished. Therefore whoever relaxes one of the least of these commandments and teaches others to do the same will be called least in the kingdom of heaven, but whoever does them and teaches them will be called great in the kingdom of heaven (Matt. 5:17-19)."
   but I also had trouble with the apostle Paul, that great

messenger of mercy and grace, who said in Romans 7:12 –

" . . . the law is holy, and the commandment is holy and righteous and good."

In my zeal to avoid legalism, I found myself in conflict with Grace Incarnate and his chief apostolic theologian! I realized I needed to revise my own unbalanced view.

What is legalism, this thing I so much feared and wanted to avoid when I was young? All seminary students talked about it, but did anyone actually know what it was? I think not. Twenty-six years after leaving seminary, I and some of my colleagues in the Edmonton Vineyard churches were engaged in a conversation with a man we had brought in as a guest speaker, a highly prophetic man with a broad ministry throughout the Body of Christ. Someone in our group other than I expressed to him some grave concern about the dangers of legalism. I was so eager to hear his response. He smiled, then chuckled and said, "The church today is so far from legalism, we are in danger of all becoming libertines!" I was a little surprised to hear him speak so strongly like that, but I was coming to the same conclusion myself.

I had been studying II Thessalonians 2:1-12 where Paul talks about *the man of lawlessness* because I had run into so much teaching in certain pockets of the church about the coming of the Antichrist, which has caused some people to focus on the future appearance of some intensely evil individual. So who is the Antichrist, and who is this man of lawlessness? Are they the same? I quickly discovered that the term *Antichrist* never appears in the book of Revelation as some suppose, and the apostle John refers to "*many* antichrists (I John 2:18)", which is plural, and to "*the spirit of* the antichrist, which you heard was coming and *now is in the world already* (I John 4:3, *emphasis mine*)." Not only is the coming antichrist spirit in the world already, but most people wouldn't be able to identify him by his evil function, namely, to deny that Jesus Christ has come in the flesh (See I John 4:1-3).

As I was studying what Paul says about *the man of lawlessness*, I was coming to the conclusion that he was not talking about an individual, but about a certain manifestation of corporate humanity, such as we would talk about Israel as a messianic type in the Old Testament, the *One New Man* in Ephesians 2:15, *the Man of Reason* during the enlightenment, *the Renaissance Man* during the Renaissance, or *Modern Man* during the period of modernism.

As I have looked around at our current society, I've thought that what we're seeing is the emergence of the man of lawlessness. It's his time. He rises up in full stature to take glory to himself. The harvest of wickedness appears to be coming to full maturity, right alongside the harvest of righteousness. This corporate man of lawlessness is characterized by rebellion, destruction, playing God and proclaiming himself to be God, finding power in demonic energy, and practicing wicked deception that is effective with all "those who refuse to love the truth and so be saved (V. 10)." The end result, according to Paul, is that God gives them a snout full of what they want and actively sends upon them "a strong delusion so that they may believe what is false, in order that all may be condemned who did not believe the truth but had pleasure in unrighteousness [Greek: *adikia* - that which is out of line with the will of God] II Thess. 2:11, 12)."

So we need to avoid a pit on either side of the road. On one side is the pit of lawlessness. On the other side is the pit of legalism. The crown of the road might be called "the radical middle" because it takes considerable wisdom, grace, and maturity to live in the tension between those two extremes.

Once again, what is legalism? Legalism is like any other "ism" – you build your whole life around a particular philosophy, whether it is communism, capitalism, humanism, feminism, or egalitarianism. Legalism is the conviction that one is saved, or made right with God, by keeping the law of God perfectly in the strength of one's self. In Philippians 3:3, Paul called it "putting confidence in the flesh." Human performance under the law is everything. The Pharisees of Jesus' day were legalists in the purest sense of the word, and He was compelled to show them their incapability of doing what they professed. Now I am sure that there are some legalists in the church, but most of the people I know are more on the side of sinning all the more that grace may abound (Romans 6:1)!

What eventually became clear to me is that the law is good because it expresses the will of God. So simple.

The law is not alien to God, who is love, nor is He, in His mercy, opposed to it. *The law of God is the will of God!* The flesh, of course, is at enmity with the will of God, and when the will of God is proclaimed, the flesh will instinctively react with "That's legalism! Don't judge me!"

When I was almost 19 years old, after one year of college and several years before seminary, I was in a deep existential crisis that led to a spiritual awakening. I had gone seriously astray, and with an awakened conscience, I now wanted to come back to the Lord and walk in His ways, something I was not fully accustomed to doing! I had been living a life of compromise. I prayed as I never had before, surrendering my life.

It was an unforgettable encounter while driving my big work truck at 2:00 in the morning. One of my 13 year old twin sisters had just been killed 15 hours before in a drowning accident. As I headed toward home, there was nothing left to do but reflect on the shocking events of the day, and this life-altering loss. Suddenly, I was sobbing uncontrollably. I was completely undone. Nothing is more sobering than death. I needed the Lord, and I knew it. I couldn't afford to go on playing games with Him. I knew I needed to come to him on His terms, not my own. I was doing serious business with God who is both a consuming fire and my deliverer from death and hell. Can you feel the truth in that great paradox?

From that day on, and for many years afterward, I prayed this simple prayer each day:
"O Lord, show me your will.
Help me to love your will with all my heart
and to do it with all my strength!"
That's kind of the essence of Psalm 119, the longest Psalm in the Bible, where the psalmist expresses his love for the word of the Lord, his Law, commandments, and statutes. What a ridiculous, self-defeating contradiction that I, a lover of God's will, should years later fall into a crowd of antinomians!

I further came to realize that the Law of the Lord not only reveals His will, but it also exposes everything in my life that is out of line with his will. Of course! Why wouldn't it? The function of the Law is to let me know when I'm missing the mark (Romans 3:20). And when I miss the mark, that good and holy Law *necessitates* Christ! I would not know my need for forgiveness, correction, restoration, and spiritual empowerment apart from His Law, the revelation of his will. The good news is that mercy and grace abound in Jesus. But who needs good news if there is no problem? Jesus was speaking with sarcastic humor when he said to the Pharisees, "Those who are well have no need of a physician, but those who are sick (Matt. 9:12, Mark 2:17, Luke 5:31)." He had taken their vital signs and found them wanting, but they would have none of it. *If we call that which is sick both wholesome and healthy, we reject the healing hand of the Great Physician.* We nullify the grace of God, and make the death of Christ of no effect (cf. Gal. 2:21).

Among those in the church who defend and advocate same sex marriage, there is always an attempt to say the law in Leviticus 18:22 and 20:13 against a man "lying with a man as with a woman" is merely a matter of ritual uncleanness that doesn't really apply to us today. In other words, it's not even a minor offense, but no offense to God at all. Furthermore, they say that if this law still does apply to us today, what about all the other prohibitions that occur alongside this one in the text? What about lending money at interest? Since our current economy is built on this practice, it must be okay. "Everybody does it." Or what about eating shellfish, like lobster? We all do that too. Why embrace one prescription, and ignore another? They ask, "Where is the logical consistency?"

I have two things to say to that. The first is that not all actions have the same consequences. Some have light consequences. For example, nutritionists now tell us that there is great wisdom in avoiding the consumption of crustaceans, which are bottom-feeders. But if one must indulge this appetite for shellfish, they advise great moderation in the interest of better health. And as for lending money at interest, and the other side of the transaction – borrowing with interest, has no one ever heard of the monetary collapse of the Weimar Republic in November of 1923 because of borrowed money and the unrestrained printing of fiat currency – the very thing we see happening right now all over the world? Maybe we should have paid more attention to these laws which express God's best desires for our temporal and eternal welfare. God provides an alternative to the potential evils of lending and borrowing with interest. There is the option of *giving* to the poor, because those who give to the poor lend to the Lord. And I can personally attest that He pays handsome interest, especially when His heart for mercy is personally satisfied!

The second thing I have to say is that other actions have huge consequences. Under the Old Covenant, the infractions involving sexual immorality and sexual perversion required the death penalty. Eating shellfish did not. Furthermore, in the New Covenant, the dietary restrictions are lifted from the followers of Christ, especially from the Gentile followers, but the sins of sexual immorality still demand strong measures of discipline for both Jews and Greeks. In I Corinthians 5, where a man was sleeping with his father's wife, Paul says "I handed him over to Satan" in a radical attempt to bring him to repentance and restoration. He talks about the destruction of this man's flesh "so that his spirit may be saved in the day of the Lord (v. 5)!"

Does it really work that way? I have heard so many stories, and have witnessed a couple myself, where men have contracted A.I.D.S. through homosexual intercourse (Does Romans 1:27 apply here? ". . . men committing shameless acts with men *and receiving in themselves the due penalty for their error* [emphasis mine]") but then came to repentance and died full of faith and hope in the mercy of Jesus Christ and His promise of resurrection from the dead.

Let me say that I am fully aware that innocent people can contract A.I.D.S. in other ways such as through blood transfusions. We had a woman in our congregation who was HIV positive because of a blood transfusion given during a surgery. We prayed over her many times for healing, and she was eventually healed of this condition quite dramatically at a conference.

It concerns me that so many of my friends are rushing ahead and seeking to justify the practice of same-sex marriage, rather than continue to ask the hard questions about it. Why the hurry? This has to be the most massive cultural shift in history, attempting to toss off thousands of years of commonly held beliefs about sexual morality. Very few of us have even had a thoughtful, well-balanced discussion about this yet, and there are obvious attempts to quell such discussion and intimidate the populace into silence. With too many, I fear, the conclusions have already been reached on the basis of one-sided arguments, the decisions have already been made, and they are already at the stage of asking how we implement these new perspectives on human sexuality. I say that simply because there is now a preponderance of books advocating same-sex marriage along with *different sexualities*, with little to no references that speak about the healing of divergent sexual identities and practices. Where are the references to the extensive work and writings of Andy Comiskey, Leanne Payne, and the Sandfords (John, Paula, Loren, and Mark) of Elijah

House Ministries? Thus far, the writings seem unbalanced and one-sided, which has compelled me to respond with something from the other side of this issue.

I have been somewhat dismayed to discover that the current theological arguments for same-sex marriage are all the same ones presented to me more than 30 years ago by the homosexual pastor of the Metropolitan Community Church (MCC) in our city, Edmonton, Alberta. He had heard about our ministry with homosexuals and came to our Sunday service to meet me, hear me speak, and experience our fellowship. After the service, he introduced himself to me and we had a brief, but cordial conversation. Then he asked if he could send me some information which he would like me to read. I said I would be happy to receive it. A week later, a large envelope arrived in the mail, and I sat down and read the entire document, which wasn't more than a dozen pages. It was essentially a theological apologetic for embracing homosexuality as an acceptable alternative lifestyle. The writers offered their interpretation of the Leviticus passages in the holiness code, then went through all the New Testament passages that speak about homosexual activity offering their variant interpretations of each text. But I especially remember how that particular document dealt with "the sin of Sodom and Gomorrah."

Have you carefully studied the story lately? According to Genesis 19, all the men of Sodom, young and old, to the last man, demanded that Lot send out his visitors so that the men of the city could *know* them. The writers of the MCC document then fault the men of Sodom, not for their sexual perversion, but for their *inhospitality*. I sat in my chair and said quietly to myself, "You've got to be kidding." Wanting to meet and get to know your close neighbor's out-of-town guests would be, in my neighborhood, an act of hospitality, not inhospitality. But demanding to have group sex with them would be sexual abuse, violence and perversion of the worst sort. Merely calling it *inhospitality* is minimalization of the highest order.

And then the writers of the document insisted that, according to Ezekiel 16:49-50, Sodom and Gomorrah were destroyed for having wealth but turning a blind eye to the poor and needy. No doubt, that's a very serious issue, especially during that period of history! God required mercy for the widow, the orphan, and the sojourner whose very survival depended on it.

But I find it curious that the Metropolitan Community Church cited the reason for Sodom's destruction by quoting a prophet living in Babylon around 600 B.C. *to the exclusion of* what the Genesis account itself says about the judgment from heaven that took place roughly 1,400 years earlier. Both Genesis and Ezekiel need to be taken into account. According to Genesis 18:20, the Lord destroyed Sodom because "the outcry against Sodom and Gomorrah is great and their sin is very grave" (Are we really talking only about inhospitality and social inequality here, as if gross sexual immorality is not a factor as well?) and because he could not find ten righteous men in the city. Remember, before we are told of the complete destruction of Sodom, we are told that *every last man in the city, young and old*, was in the crowd that day, demanding to sexually violate the messengers of God. Sodom was destroyed *because God couldn't find 10 righteous men*. See also Jude 7! We don't need to look any further than the immediate context within Genesis, or find some other explanation! This closely parallels the reason for Noah's flood in Genesis 6:5:

"The LORD saw that the wickedness of man was great in the earth

and that *every imagination of the thoughts of his heart*

was only evil continually (RSV, emphasis mine)."

The very fact that the Lord singles out Sodom for utter destruction *from heaven* would indicate the extreme nature of their sin and the extreme nature of his wrath against it. Where else does he do that in Scripture? This is extra-ordinary in the clearest sense of that word!

Further to this is the fact that Moses, in Deuteronomy 32:31-33, identifies Sodom and Gomorrah as the archetype of Baalism and all the enemies of God by using the cultural symbol of the fertility cults: serpents.

> For their rock is not as our Rock;
> our enemies are by themselves.
> For their vine comes from the vine of Sodom
> and from the fields of Gomorrah;
> their grapes are grapes of poison;
> their clusters are bitter;
> their wine is the poison of serpents
> and the cruel venom of asps.

When the defense of same sex marriage as an acceptable alternative lifestyle moves to the New Testament, some writers like to contend that Jesus didn't have one word to say about homosexuality. First of all, that's a logical fallacy called the *argument from silence.* It's impossible to prove. It is true we have no *recorded* words of Jesus speaking *explicitly* about homosexuality. However, William R. Loader, who has written more than half a dozen books on sexuality in the Scriptures, thinks it very probable that in Mark 9:42-48 Jesus is referring to pederasty, the all-too-common practice in the Roman empire of males having small boys around for sexual gratification.[18]

42 "If any of you *put a stumbling block* (Greek: *skandalizo*) before one of these little ones who believe in me, it would be better for you if a great millstone were hung around your neck and you were thrown into the sea. 43 If your hand causes you to stumble, cut it off; it is better for you to enter life maimed than to have two hands and to go to hell, to the unquenchable fire. 45 And if your foot causes you to stumble, cut it off; it is better for you to enter life lame than to have two feet and to be thrown into hell. 47 And if your eye causes you to stumble, tear it out; it is better for you to enter the kingdom of God with one eye than to have two eyes and to be thrown into hell, 48 where their worm never dies, and the fire is never quenched (NRSV).

The key word here in the Greek text is *skandalizo*, which means *to cause someone to stumble so as to lose their faith*. Ask yourself, "How many things are there that adults, authority figures, who have the responsibility to represent God to little children – how many things can they do that would actually cause children to stumble and lose their faith in God?" Frankly, I don't think there are many. Children can be quite resilient. I have seen children from some very troubled homes continue to persist in their faith in God, even attending Sunday school and church on their own. But sexual abuse from a trusted adult seems to completely obscure the heart of God.

In recent years here in Canada, it has become apparent that one of the greatest scars on the soul of our First Nations People is the sexual abuse that took place in the church-owned residential schools that the government demanded aboriginal children attend. When our intercessors pray for the healing of our land, these are the things over which they weep and wail.

Considering the extreme consequences of the fires of hell that Jesus himself spells out, Loader's interpretation makes the most sense to me. How can we not sense the wrath of God in His words? I have counselled men who were the victims of pederasty and the resulting spiritual and psychological damage they endure puts it right up there alongside the effects of satanic ritualistic abuse. The hell they experience for the rest of their lives and the things they do to kill the pain are almost beyond comprehension. Thank God, I lived to see the day when there is deep and lasting healing, even for that, but there are so few who know how to minister at that level of deepest wounding.

In an article entitled "Did Jesus Talk About Homosexuality?", New Testament scholar Scot McKnight suggests the strong possibility that Jesus also alludes to homosexuality in Matthew 11:7-9.

7 As they went away, Jesus began to speak to the crowds

concerning John: "What did you go out into the wilderness to see? A reed shaken by the wind? 8 What then did you go out to see? A man dressed *in soft clothing* [Grk: *en malakois*]? Behold, those who wear soft clothing are in kings' houses. 9 What then did you go out to see? A prophet? Yes, I tell you, and more than a prophet. (ESV, *emphasis mine*)

This Greek term, *malakos (meaning* soft, submissive, compliant), refers to "the receptive partner in same-sex relations" and occurs in I Cor. 6:9-10 –

9 Do you not know that wrongdoers will not inherit the kingdom of God? Do not be deceived! Fornicators, idolaters, adulterers, *male prostitutes (malakoi)*, sodomites, 10 thieves, the greedy, drunkards, revilers, robbers – none of these will inherit the kingdom of God (NRSV).

It is a well-established fact that Roman rulers kept young men in their private dwellings for their sexual pleasure. Jesus appears to be making a very subtle but powerful contrast here between John, who represents Elijah,[19] the one who faced off against Jezebel and the prophets of Baal, and all those who are enslaved, prostituted, to the rulers of this age. John's prophetic ministry is bold and without compromise, and he speaks out against sexual sin just as Elijah did – which ultimately led to his beheading at the hands of Herod.

The term that Jesus *did* use in speaking out against sexual sin, *porneia*, occurs in Matthew 5:32, 15:19 and 19:9, and is consistently translated as *sexual immorality*. Sexual immorality is a broad and general term that includes every kind of sexual activity outside of the creator's intended design for man. While someone of our time and culture, possibly looking for moral loopholes, might wonder what the term *porneia* may or may not include, no Jew in the days of Jesus would have such a thought. First off, Jesus Himself was a Torah-observant Jewish Rabbi. The Jewish mind, profoundly shaped by the Torah, would immediately reference Leviticus 18 that sets the chosen people apart from all the pagan

gentiles by prohibiting sexual relations with:
 close relatives (18:6)
 parents (18:7) and the spouses of parents (18:8)
 siblings (18:9, 11)
 spouses of one's children or their children (18:10)
 aunts [and uncles] or their spouses (18:12-14)
 children by law (18:15)
 sisters-in-law [and brothers-in-law](18:16)
 a woman and her daughter and her children (18:17)
 women during menstruation (18:19)
 neighbor's wife (18:20)
 same-sex relations (18:22)
 and animals (18:23).[20]

In the current debate over sexual conduct, we commonly see the advocates of same-sex marriage set the apostles over against Jesus, as if Jesus were at odds with his own apostles. Even if it were true that Jesus had not one word to say about homosexuality, which I don't think is true, as I've tried to demonstrate, the argument from silence needs to be exposed as a ruse. The apostle John said, John 21:25, "Now there are also many other things that Jesus did. Were every one of them to be written, I suppose that the world itself could not contain the books that would be written."

But according to the books that *were* written, Jesus *did* say,
 "Do not think that I have come to abolish the Law or the Prophets; I have not come to abolish them but to fulfill them. For truly, I say to you, until heaven and earth pass away, not an iota, not a dot, will pass from the Law until all is accomplished. Therefore whoever relaxes one of the least of these commandments and teaches others to do the same will be called least in the kingdom of heaven, but whoever does them and teaches them will be called great in the kingdom of heaven (Matt. 5:17-19)."
 And also in Luke 16:17,
 "But it is easier for heaven and earth to pass away than for one dot of the Law to become void."

Where the Law has already spoken, Jesus embodies that righteousness, and identifies with it fully. Jesus never distanced himself from the Law. He only reinforced it, or offered clarity and a better understanding of the expressed will of God. For example, He said, "The Sabbath is made for man, not man for the Sabbath." "You have heard it said of old, do not commit adultery. But I say unto you . . ."

Although Jesus *may not* have spoken specifically about homosexual acts, he did speak about sexual immorality (*porneia*), which broadly covers every form of sexual activity, contrary to the design and will of God, that defiles us and those around us. As we said previously, the Jews of Jesus' day would have immediately referenced Leviticus 18 as the long list for people who weren't sure!

"But what comes out of the mouth proceeds from the heart, and this defiles a person. For out of the heart come evil thoughts, murder, adultery, sexual immorality, theft, false witness, slander. These are what defile a person. But to eat with unwashed hands does not defile anyone. (Matthew 15:18-20)."

The debate then moves to the many passages in the New Testament that warn us about every manner of sin that can destroy our lives or rob us of our spiritual inheritance in the Kingdom. Prominent in all these lists are different manifestations of sexual immorality, which usually appear at the beginning of the lists. I think there is a reason for listing them first, but I'll save that for later. At the head of the list in I Corinthians 6 is idolatry (which often involved temple prostitution), adultery, and men who practice homosexuality.

"Or do you not know that the unrighteous will not inherit the kingdom of God? Do not be deceived: neither the sexually immoral, nor idolaters, nor adulterers, nor men who practice homosexuality, nor thieves, nor greedy, nor drunkards, nor revilers, nor swindlers will inherit the Kingdom of God. And such were some of you. But you were washed, you were sanctified, you were justified in the name of the Lord Jesus Christ and by the Spirit of our God (I Cor. 6:9-11)."

Invariably, there is quibbling about the phrase, "men who practice homosexuality," which is a translation of a single compound Greek word, *arsenokoitai*. The first part of the word, *arsen*, is a relatively uncommon word for man. The most common words for man in Greek are *aner* (man, or husband) and *anthropos* (generic man, or mankind, as distinct from animals) *Arsen* is unique in that it denotes a male in sexual differentiation from a female.[21] The word carries a heightened awareness of sexuality. And the second part, *koite*, is a word that can either denote the marital bed or the sexual conjugation that takes place there. It is also a word that is translated, in some contexts, as sexual immorality. It is interesting that the word closely corresponds to the Latin (the language of the Roman Empire at that time) *coitus*, which means having come together sexually. It is protested that the term *arsenokoitai* is rare and the meaning is not clear. You decide. In my opinion, the immediate context seems to justify the rendering of *arsenokoitai* as *men who practice homosexuality* to be both likely and logical. It's not the same kind of sexual immorality as fornication, adultery, bestiality, or incest and apparently requires some further articulation.

I suppose what troubles me the most is the fact that so many of the same-sex marriage proponents spend so much energy on the first part of this I Corinthians 6 passage trying to convince us that the meaning of this one word is uncertain and therefore irrelevant, rather than expounding on the latter part of this oft-cited verse: "And such were some of you!"

The first time I read that and actually understood what Paul was saying, I nearly jumped out of my own skin! The Corinthian church consisted of many people who had lived lives of significant immorality and degradation, but had undergone a radical transformation by the mercy and the grace of God! What can be more exciting that a dramatically transformed life? This stuff gives credence to the central doctrine of the church, resurrection from the dead! All things are possible with God!

Evidently, they had experienced a power encounter with the living God through His church. Although the text only hints at it, they had gone through some kind of inner healing experience. "You were washed!" He doesn't name the agent of that washing, but whether it was with the physical waters of baptism or the figurative blood of Christ, such a thing would only come in response to a renunciation of the devil and all his works, a full confession of sin, and the evidence of repentance.

Then Paul says, "You were sanctified!" In other words, you were discipled into a life *set apart* for the service of God. With some knowledge of the catechetical process in the early church, I would say this indicates a path of discipleship where people are mentored to spiritual maturity so as to walk no longer according to the flesh, but according to the spirit.

Then Paul says, "You were justified!" This says to me that they had come into full identification with Jesus, the only *truly just man* on the face of the earth. By that I mean that Jesus was *fully aligned* with the will of God. "I have been crucified with Christ. It is no longer I who live, but Christ who lives in me (Gal. 2:20)." Such a radical identification produces an equally radical re-alignment with the will and purposes of God.

"Such were some of you" has given way to a washed-sanctified-justified people of God.[22] "Therefore, if anyone is in Christ, he is a new creation. The old has passed away; behold, the new has come (II Cor. 5:17)!"

I've said ever since, "God, that's the kind of church I want to pastor. I don't want to babysit people who think they need no healing. I want to pastor people who are at least as broken as I am, people who can demonstrate the power of the gospel of the kingdom by their changed lives!" And He has been faithful to answer that prayer. I love our local church – a healing community of wounded healers in process. It's as real as it can be.

Let's turn our attention now to the interpretation of Romans 1:18-32. As Peter says in his book, " . . . one passage stood above all others in keeping me from a full acceptance of homosexual union–Romans 1:26-27."[23] Rather than cite only those two verses, let me reproduce more of the context, which begins with an incredibly sobering word about the wrath of God, something we hardly ever talk about these days:

"For I am not ashamed of the gospel, for it is the power of God for salvation to everyone who believes, to the Jew first and also to the Greek. For in it the righteousness of God is revealed from faith to faith, as it is written, "The righteous shall live by faith." *For the wrath of God is revealed from heaven against all ungodliness and unrighteousness of men*, who by their unrighteousness suppress the truth. For what can be known about God is plain to them, because God has shown it to them. For his invisible attributes, namely, his eternal power and divine nature, have been clearly perceived, ever since the creation of the world, in the things that have been made. So they are without excuse. For although they knew God, they did not honor him as God or give thanks to him, but they became futile in their thinking, and their foolish hearts were darkened. Claiming to be wise, they became fools, and exchanged the glory of the immortal God for images resembling mortal man and birds and animals and creeping things.

Therefore God gave them up in the lusts of their hearts to impurity, to the dishonoring of their bodies among themselves, because they exchanged the truth about God for a lie and worshipped and served the creature rather than the creator, who is blessed forever! Amen.

For this reason God gave them up to dishonourable passions. For their women exchanged natural relations for those that are contrary to nature; and the men likewise gave up natural relations with women and were consumed with passion for one another, men committing shameless acts with men and receiving in themselves the due penalty for their error.

And since they did not see fit to acknowledge God, God gave them up to a debased mind to do what ought not to be done. They were filled with all manner of unrighteousness, evil, covetousness, malice. They are full of envy, murder, strife, deceit, maliciousness. They are gossips, slanderers, haters of God, insolent, haughty, boastful, inventors of evil, disobedient to parents, foolish, faithless, heartless, ruthless. Though they know God's decree that those who practice such things deserve to die, they not only do them but give approval to those who practice them (Romans 1:16-32, ESV, italics mine)."

I think that my friend, Peter, rightly points out that this passage describes the practices of the gentiles, whom we might call the ungodly, the heathen. There is an increase of wickedness. Things get progressively worse. And God gives them up. He lets sin run its course, until people experience the full consequences of their self-willed behavior.

Where I disagree is when Peter says,
" . . . people are pushing beyond intuitive barriers, pressing toward more and more outrageous behaviors. They are experimenting sexually and pushing past the place that feels natural to them in order to try for more and more sensual satisfaction[24]."

and then goes on to say,

"I am now convinced that the homosexuality that Paul is writing about is of the nature that I've described above. It refers to heterosexual people who are pressing past their intuitive sexual orientation in order to strive for greater and greater sensual experience.

It has nothing to do with the minority of people who find that they have always and only been oriented toward their own gender, or toward those who realize that they are same-gender attracted as their sexuality matures.[25]"

I am fully aware of the fact that there are people who commit homosexual acts who do not identify themselves as homosexuals, so I always distinguish between homosexual activity and homosexual identity. This is common among men in situations where large male populations are deprived of female companionship for extended periods of time, such as in the military, or in prison. We see this degradation depicted in the movie, *The Shawshank Redemption*. Many, when released from these circumstances, discontinue their homosexual acts. I also know from my extensive experience as a pastoral counsellor that a few people who strongly self-identify themselves as homosexual have never committed a homosexual act. Furthermore, I know from my counselling experience that many who self-identify with homosexuality began to do so after they were sexually molested, abused, or raped.

So – objectively speaking, what are "intuitive barriers" "intuitive sexual orientation" or "the place that feels *natural?*" This implies that all parties are stable, mature, and completely free from any confusion about sexual identity. In a natural order where everything in creation is fallen and distorted, *arguing from that which is "natural" is meaningless*. The only thing that is "natural" is our brokenness, and that we have all been deceived by the devil, and are therefore self-deceived!

I mostly agree with Peter that Romans 1 builds up to the following chapter, which is a warning to the Jewish-Gentile church not to assume moral superiority and pass judgment on such people, which is so easy to do. Much of the church of our day is certainly guilty of that. Unfortunately, those who carry the placards that say, "All homosexuals are going to hell" usually get on the nightly news of international television. No wonder the world doesn't see the church as the healing community we read about in the New Testament! Judgment blinds us to our own weakness and predisposition to sin, and neutralizes us as the missionary enterprise of God.

I think the point is that Romans 1 is not just a current picture of what the pagans of the Roman Empire do, but this is a history of all mankind, and also a picture of what the chosen people of God have historically done. Over hundreds of years, Israel consistently fell into the ways of the idolatrous gentiles around them until we read this in II Chronicles 36:15, 16:

"The LORD, the God of their fathers, sent persistently to them by his messengers, because he had compassion on his people and on his dwelling place. But they kept mocking the messengers of God, despising his words and scoffing at his prophets, until the wrath of the LORD rose against his people, *until there was no remedy* (ESV, italics mine)."

What impresses me most about Romans 1 and 2 is that God's intended orientation for human behavior is not what is "intuitive" or "feels natural", but what reflects the nature and glory of the Creator! God Himself is at the centre of this text. Orientation is always and only in relationship to Him. He is true north. God has plainly revealed Himself in His nature and attributes as the creator of all that is. He is the One who has created us in His own image to reflect His glory. So really, what do we know about our creator, the author of life, the invisible God? He who encompasses in His own being the fullness of masculinity and femininity creates us as male and female and tells us to use our reproductive capacities to multiply and fill the earth. That's a shorthand way of saying He is all about creation, and engaging our cooperation in that activity. Everything we say and do was intended to be a pure expression of Him. Slow down and think deeply on this. This is absolutely critical. *Creatio* (creation). *Imago Dei* (image of God). These two things are the foundation for all that follows.

And he apparently gets pretty angry when we mess with any of that, especially the essential components of maleness, femaleness, and procreation. "Pretty angry" is actually a serious understatement. The passage under consideration actually begins with *wrath*, which is far stronger than anger. It's in a different class altogether. The word *wrath* is used four times in Romans 1:8; 2:5 and 2:8. I've learned from my theological studies that wrath, when referring to the wrath of God, is an extreme term. It's different from harsh discipline. God disciplines those whom he loves. Discipline can mean 400 years in Egypt, or 40 years in the wilderness, or 70 years in Babylon. But wrath is reserved for final judgment. It comes when discipline no longer works. When wrath comes, it's too late. There is no longer any opportunity to repent. It's game over, lights out!

The great flood in the days of Noah, Genesis 6 - 8, is no doubt the clearest biblical type of the wrath of God. God's "never again" declaration in Genesis 8:21 could seem to imply that the Lord Himself was horrified at the massive destruction, even though He saw it as necessary to cleanse His creation of the unmitigated corruption.

The Day of Wrath and the Day of Judgment are one and the same. It is something that has been stored up for a long, long time. Wrath is the destruction of everything in creation that gives a distorted view of God and suppresses the truth about God.

I don't enjoy talking about wrath. I don't think God does either. II Peter 3:9 says that God is "not willing that any should perish, but that all should reach repentance." But I hear in Romans 1 a warning louder and more shrill than an air raid siren. Some are concerned about not hurting the feelings of people who claim lesbian, gay, bi-sexual, or transgendered as their sexual identity. I don't want to hurt or shame them either, and the many ones I've befriended soon discovered that. But I'm more concerned about dishonoring God, my Father, who has given me new life and a new identity in Christ. I'm appealing to all who are still my friends to slow down, because the danger of doing the right things for the wrong reasons right now is grave, especially in the light of the healing I've seen firsthand, and to which I now bear witness.

We need to be careful that we are not speaking mercy where God Himself is speaking wrath. I believe that was the message of Dietrich Bonhoeffer in *The Cost of Discipleship* when he expounded on the notion of "cheap grace."

Some think we've talked about this long enough, but I believe I have been given some things to say that haven't yet been heard.

THE STRONG DELUSION

There is a tremendous storm brewing, both in the natural realm and in the realm of the spirit. There is no need right now to talk about dramatic climate change and the upheaval and chaos in the weather where we live. We're doing that every day. I intend to speak of the spiritual storm. The physical always points to the spiritual, so let's talk about the spiritual.

One major indication of the spiritual storm that is equal to the melting of a polar ice cap, or the reversing of the north and south polarity of the earth, is what is happening right now in the church over the issue of same sex marriage. The seeds of the storm started with the sexual revolution of the sixties, but it has been picking up energy at an exponential rate. It took some form with the promotion of the homosexual agenda in some of the historic, mainline denominations. It progressed to the ordination of practicing homosexuals in those same denominations. Now we have a few evangelical (as distinct from mainline denominational) pastors, authors, and academics advocating the support of same sex marriage within the evangelical church. That's like getting a blizzard and 15 feet of snow in a place where it's never snowed before!

Just like a cold front colliding with a warm front to set off a lightning and thunderstorm that spawns tornadoes, so there is extreme polarization building over this issue in the evangelical church. There is little doubt in my mind that there will be gut-wrenching divisions and horrible mental, emotional, and spiritual destruction. I wish it were not so. But in the physical realm, they say storms are necessary to restore nature to balance and order. No doubt, the spiritual realm parallels that reality. It would be wise to find the Lord as your shelter and hiding place if you want to survive this one.

I long for the appearing of our God and Savior, Jesus the Messiah, don't you? I hope we recognize him when He comes. So few did the first time. They were looking for a Messiah who would come to judge and overthrow the world system. Instead, He came as a sacrificial lamb so that people could be saved, healed, and delivered through His suffering, death, and resurrection. Such love! Now that we know Him as our loving and healing savior, what a shock it would be to see him come the second time as a judge.

During my eight years in Lutheran colleges and seminary, hundreds of young men used to attend daily chapel and chant with great power the ancient *Te Deum Laudamus,* Latin for "We praise you, O God." Near the end of that magnificent plainsong hymn we sang, "We believe that Thou shalt come to be our judge." It's the only part I didn't like. It made me shudder a bit. I had some significant fear of judgment. Holy Jesus, meek and mild – where are you now?

But I think most of us have gotten over that. Who talks about judgment these days? Who even believes in Hell anymore? We now know that Jesus is our buddy and He loves everybody. Unconditionally – which makes the three ecumenical creeds an embarrassment to some people because they all say we believe that "He shall come to judge the living and the dead."

I've changed over the years. I no longer fear judgment the way I did. I stand in awe of it, but I don't fear punishment. I believe that I have passed from judgment to life. My Great High Priest has cleansed my conscience. That's a good thing. Furthermore, I understand judgment better. It means "to put everything right." I ache over all the corruption and injustice in this world that no one can seem to do anything about. God alone is our only hope. He will put everything right. There is a tremendous upside! There will be rewards for faithfulness and endurance! There will be an end to our suffering and tears. Sickness and death will be no more. But God Himself will deal decisively, once and for all, with all that is *genuinely* evil. I only say *genuinely* evil because of Isaiah 5:20 –

". . . Woe to those who call evil good, and good evil . . ."

According to Genesis 2:17, only God can say what is truly good and evil.

Psalm 98 ends with these words,

7 Let the sea roar, and all that fills it;
the world and those who dwell in it!
8 Let the rivers clap their hands;
let the hills sing for joy together
9 before the Lord, for he comes
to judge the earth.
He will judge the world with righteousness,
and the peoples with equity.

Judgment is something to roar, and clap, and sing about!

The whole creation has been groaning in travail for that day!

Justice at last!

I am more convinced than ever that the second coming, the Day of the Lord is near. With an eye on the words of Jesus about that day, is there anything that does not point to it? Signs in the heavens above and on the earth beneath. Increased lawlessness and worldwide terrorism. Massive deception. The continual threat of imminent global financial collapse, and nuclear weapons in the hands of madmen.

But what persuades me more than anything else of coming judgment is what Paul speaks prophetically in II Thessalonians 2:1-12. I know that I spoke earlier in the book about this passage, and forgive me if I seem to belabour it, but I have a few additional observations to make.

2 Now concerning the coming of our Lord Jesus Christ and our

being gathered together to him, we ask you, brothers, 2 not to be quickly shaken in mind or alarmed, either by a spirit or a spoken word, or a letter seeming to be from us, to the effect that the day of the Lord has come. 3 Let no one deceive you in any way. For that day will not come, unless the rebellion comes first, and the man of lawlessness is revealed, the son of destruction, 4 who opposes and exalts himself against every so-called god or object of worship, so that he takes his seat in the temple of God, proclaiming himself to be God. 5 Do you not remember that when I was still with you I told you these things? 6 And you know what is restraining him now so that he may be revealed in his time. 7 For the mystery of lawlessness is already at work. Only he who now restrains it will do so until he is out of the way. 8 And then the lawless one will be revealed, whom the Lord Jesus will kill with the breath of his mouth and bring to nothing by the appearance of his coming. 9 The coming of the lawless one is by the activity of Satan with all power and false signs and wonders, 10 and with all wicked deception for those who are perishing, because they refused to love the truth and so be saved. 11 Therefore God sends them a strong delusion, so that they may believe what is false, 12 in order that all may be condemned who did not believe the truth but had pleasure in unrighteousness.

I've been fascinated by this scripture for a long time. He says the Day of the Lord will not come until the rebellion comes first and the man of lawlessness is revealed. Is he talking about rebellion against the law of the *land*, or the law of the *Lord*? It is becoming increasingly clear that there is a widening gap between the Law of the Lord and the law of the land. Divine authority for human morality is being supplanted with the relative morality of secular humanism. Is he merely talking about civil lawlessness? Because if he is, human society is shot through with lawlessness, and even the governments of the world violate their own constitutions, and the rights of their own citizens. But more to the point is the widespread manifestation of lawlessness against God in the church, particularly in all aspects of sexual morality. When lawlessness is so widespread, that tells me we're seeing *the man of lawlessness*. He's not a single person as some suppose, but a corporate man, the opposite of the "One New Man in Christ" that Paul talks about in Ephesians 2:15.

Lawlessness in the natural realm points to lawlessness in the spiritual, and I think this apostle, who says in Romans 7:12 "So the law is holy, and the commandment is holy and righteous and good" is talking about lawlessness in relation to the Law (the Will) of God. I believe he is talking about lawlessness in the temple of God, which can be construed to refer to the Church, the Body of Christ, as well as the body of any individual member of the Church. Theologians call this antinomianism. Anti = against; nomos = law. The *rebellion* is against God Himself as He expresses His good and holy will in the Law. Now I know that saying this will raise a lot of hackles among some of my peers. They may get angry, cry "legalist!" and possibly stop reading right here.

I only come with this strong interpretation of Paul because of what Jesus Himself apparently foresaw when He said (Yes, these words again!),
    "Do not think that I have come to abolish the Law or the Prophets; I have not come to abolish them but to fulfill them. For truly, I say to you, until heaven and earth pass away, not an iota, not a dot, will pass from the Law until all is accomplished. Therefore whoever relaxes one of the least of these commandments and teaches others to do the same will be called least in the kingdom of heaven, but whoever does them and teaches them will be called great in the kingdom of heaven (Matt. 5:17-19, ESV)."

What is primarily at issue in this debate over same-sex marriage is the Law of God, especially in the book of Leviticus concerning sexual morality. The thrust of chapter 18 is God's plan to separate his chosen people from the ways of the pagan world, typified in both Egypt and Canaan. He says "Don't do as they do." And then he spells out all of the ways that they live out their lives under the spell of their demon gods. The list of things that God forbids is quite comprehensive, and includes a long list of sexual activities that all fall outside the sexual relationship of a man and woman in the covenant of marriage. Also on the list are such things as uncovering the nakedness of a woman who is menstruating, or copulating with her, or uncovering the nakedness of relatives or parents.

What is being done now with these passages is to essentially explain them away, saying they are only talking about ritual impurity, and since we're not Jews living under the old covenant, that doesn't apply to us today. Or, some say that these laws of God only apply to people who perform these sexual acts with brutality, violence, and a will to dehumanize and dominate – but not to those who are faithful, loving, and monogamous. Does that thinking work with fornication, incest, pederasty, and bestiality too?

In Leviticus 18:22, where it says, "You shall not *lie* with a male as with a woman," the word *lie* implies *mutuality* – not brutality, violence, or a will to dehumanize or dominate. It appears to correspond directly in spirit with Romans 1:27 that talks about men who were "*consumed with passion for one another.*" I am convinced that this particular argument to disqualify this text from our current culture is invalid.

In my interactions with men who have been pushed into male prostitution, or have been raped, "lying" is not the physical position that is assumed when there is the will to dehumanize or dominate! Hearing these stories have been some of the most difficult and defiling conversations I've had to sit through.

What the Leviticus text makes clear is that God judges the Gentile nations for these *unclean* activities and He promises to judge His own people in the same way if they live like the Gentiles. He says the land *vomited* the inhabitants out. What a picture! The sins of the people make the whole creation get nauseous and throw up. And then He says, the same thing will happen to you "If you follow their practices. The land will vomit you out too. (Leviticus 18:28)." And it did. Israel lost her inheritance in the land and went into captivity, from which only a remnant returned.

And then, ignoring what Jesus just said about not coming to abolish the Law, there is a further appeal to the argument that we are living under a new covenant where the Law has been replaced by grace, so it doesn't apply to us anymore. The Bible doesn't actually say that. What it *does* say is,

1 There is therefore now no condemnation for those who are in Christ Jesus. 2 For the law of the Spirit of life has set you free in Christ Jesus from the law of sin and death. 3 For God has done what the law, weakened by the flesh, could not do. By sending his own Son in the likeness of sinful flesh and for sin, he condemned sin in the flesh, 4 *in order that the righteous requirement of the law might be fulfilled in us*, who walk not according to the flesh but according to the Spirit (Rom. 8:1-4, ESV, *emphasis mine*).

Grace is not merely forgiveness for the past and anything goes in the future. Grace is God's empowering presence, His Spirit at work in us "in order that the righteous requirement of the law might be fulfilled in us." Eugene Petersen expresses that last part so clearly in *The Message:*

"The law always ended up being used as a Band-Aid on sin instead of a deep healing of it. And now what the law code asked for but we couldn't deliver is accomplished as we, instead of redoubling our own efforts, simply embrace what the Spirit is doing in us."

But if we have welcomed a spirit of lawlessness into the church, my concern is with the last verse of that quote from II Thessalonians. Lawlessness leads to wicked deception, and to a refusal to love the truth and so be saved. "Therefore God sends them a *strong delusion*, so they believe what is false, in order that all may be condemned who did not believe the truth but had pleasure in unrighteousness."

I wonder if the strong delusion is not upon us already. I'll tell you why I say that. First of all, we have been blind to a different gospel of homosexual liberty, infused with an evangelistic passion to convert society. The following was laid out in the 1980s by the National Gay Task Force.[26]

1. The first order of business is the desensitization of the American people concerning gays and gay rights.

2. Almost any behavior begins to look normal if you are exposed to it enough.

3. The main thing is to talk about gayness until the issue becomes thoroughly tiresome.

4. Where we talk is important. The visual media, film and television, are plainly the most powerful image makers in Western civilization. The average American household watches over seven hours of television daily. Those hours open a gate: the private world of straights, through which a Trojan horse might be passed. As far as desensitization is concerned, the medium is the message of normalcy.

5. Portray gays as victims. In any campaign to win over the public we must be cast as victims in need of protection, so that straights will be inclined by reflex to assume the role of the protector.

We can undercut the moral authority of homophobic churches by portraying them as antiquated backwaters badly out of step with the times.

6. At a later stage of the media campaign for gay rights, it will be time to get tough with remaining opponents. To be blunt, they must be vilified...The public must be shown images of ranting homophobes whose secondary traits and beliefs disgust Middle America. These images might include: the Klu Klux Klan demanding that gays be burnt alive or castrated; bigoted southern ministers drooling with hysterical hatred to a degree that looks both comical and deranged. These images should be combined by a method propagandists call the bracket technique.

The success of this agenda was confirmed in a recent (May 22, 2015) Gallup poll that stated "Americans think 25 percent of the population are lesbians or gay men!"[27] That's off by a factor of 6!

Secondly, many have bought the oft-repeated dogma that homosexuality is genetically pre-determined. We have been told that no one chooses to be homosexual, they are "born that way" with an inverted nature. There is no credible evidence to validate such a claim, and I will address that issue in the next chapter. Being "born that way" and *believing* one is born that way are two different things. We fallen humans are susceptible to all kinds of delusions.

As a pastoral counsellor for the past 35 years, I have seen scores of counselees who were trapped in a homosexual identity because of lies that they came to believe about themselves. Jesus helps us to understand how the devil works to steal, kill, and destroy. He tells us that the devil is a liar, and the father of lies. This agrees with the testimony of John who calls him "the deceiver of the whole world." And in the book of beginnings (Genesis) where all the seed principles are found, it's clear that it was nothing more than a lie from the devil that mankind believed and acted upon to cause the fall of mankind and the exaltation of Satan as the god of this world. John Sandford of Elijah House Ministries makes this bold statement: "The only power Satan has is the power of delusion." I wondered, "Could this possibly be true?" I tested that maxim for years and concluded that it is absolutely true. The lies of the devil have no power in themselves. They must get their power from our faith. If we believe his lies and act on them, those lies then shape and control our lives. And the only antidote for a lie is the truth.

Lies versus Truth: This is the premise behind the Immanuel approach to Theophostic Prayer Ministry, one of the approaches we have used to great effect in healing prayer. People come for healing who are crippled with painful memories. The memory is a neutral container, but it carries pain because of a lie the person has come to believe about themselves. Jesus, who says of Himself, "I am the Truth" is asked to shine His light on the enemy's lie and expose it. After he does that, then we ask Him to reveal the truth to this person through His indwelling Spirit. The truth always rings true and brings a deep transformation to one's inner being. As Jesus Himself tells us, " . . . you will know the truth, and the truth will set your free (Jn. 8:32)." Filled with the truth, the person can go back to the memory and no longer feel any emotional pain, only calm and peace. The lie has been dislodged and replaced by truth.

Lies and truth have become central to the way I see homosexuality, and how I minister freedom and healing. As Colin Cook once said, "I began to realize that I had been locked for years into a grand illusion about myself – what I call the homosexual lie."[28] John Sandford resonates with this assessment when he says that there is always a principality of delusion behind homosexuality. The Immanuel Prayer Ministry approach which I just outlined, is only one of several ways we use to disarm the lies and discover the truth about ourselves in Jesus Christ. What is ultimately life-changing for those who suffer from acute sexual identity confusion, as it is for each of us, is to fully know and appropriate our true identity in Jesus Christ. *We cannot know the truth about ourselves apart from Jesus Christ.* I promise to fully develop this insight and how to impart it in the companion *Handbook for Healing the Sexually Broken.*

The mere mention of healing for homosexuality will cause some people to call me a homophobe, so polarized is the atmosphere. Talk of healing implies a sickened condition that needs to be healed. So what's the big deal? I acknowledge that I have had, and continue to have, sickened conditions that need to be healed, and healing is a process. For example, my tendency toward workaholism is rooted in an old lie about having to prove my value more than others do. I know that people value me for what I *do* for them, and it is easy to get affirmation for that, but it is another thing to believe that I can be loved simply for who I *am*, one created in the image of God.

I can also say that I have never related deeply to another human being who did not reveal the need for some sort of healing. I think we tend to underestimate the damage we all sustained through the fall in Genesis 3. To put it another way, we fail to recognize just how far we fell. We don't have a long and detailed picture of man before the fall. We only know that he walked naked before the living God without fear or shame and that he exercised dominion over the entire created order. If we want a clearer picture of Adam before the Fall, we can only see that in Jesus, the Last Adam and the Second Man, when he walks on water, stills the wind and the waves, and takes tax money from the mouth of a fish. And then there is his undiminished glory in the love of the Father on the Mount of Transfiguration. We only get an inkling of our brokenness and depravity when we behold Him who is True Man! He is the only true measure of what is *normal* and *healthy* in God's created order!

Well, concerning a sickened condition about ones sexual identity (I had a few minor struggles of my own), I neither hate nor fear people with a homosexual identity. I feel love and compassion for those who want to be free. It is not possible to minister healing without an abundance of faith, hope, and love. And I have seen scores walk in lasting healing from sexual identity confusion. In my 45 years of ministry, this kind of healing has inspired me to persist long after most others quit, simply because I get to see the reality of the Kingdom of God on earth. I get to witness the powerful activity of our God who raises the dead.

You will notice that I have attempted in this book to refute the way many same-sex marriage advocates explain away the New Testament passages that speak about all manner of sexual immorality, including homosexual intercourse. I am speaking especially of I Corinthians 6 and Romans 1. However, I am discovering that sparring over those texts, which are very compelling for me, is quite fruitless with someone who has already staked out their position on same-sex marriage. I once heard a prophetic man say that the key to hearing clearly from

God was not to have an opinion about anything! I recognize that it's easy for any of us to become entrenched in positions that we become obligated to defend, thus rendering us unable to hear an opposing point of view, even if it comes from heaven. Lord, help us all!

Instead of sparring over individual words and verses, I believe the Lord has directed me to consider the entire biblical narrative. All the individual passages about our sexual conduct have a total biblical context, and context is everything!

The Torah, in Genesis 1:1, says, "In the beginning, **God** . . ." Everything that follows in the Scriptures, to the end of Revelation, flows out of His Being, the Great I AM, and the expression of His Divine will. It's not about us, it's about Him.

As He brings forth creation as an expression of His own nature, He does so in binaries, complimentary pairs, in other words, different (even opposing) things that work together to accomplish His purpose:

- Chaos and Order
- Light and Darkness, Sun and Moon, Evening and Morning
- Heaven and Earth
- The Sea and the Dry Land
- Plants and Animals
- Birds and Fish
- Male and Female
- and it continues on to the end:
- The New Heavens and the New Earth
- and the Marriage of Christ and His Church!
- Everything is meant to lead up to that final consummation, the Marriage Supper of the Lamb!

Consequently, God is intent on bringing to fruition His Plan for all eternity. As surely as He separated the sea from the dry land, there is a constant theme of God separating His chosen people from the idolatrous nations. Holiness is all about staying separate from the nations and their idolatry.

When God calls Abram, who was a worshipper of idols, he calls him away from Ur of the Chaldees to a new land where he will learn to walk with the Living God. When it is time for his son Isaac to marry, father Abraham sends his servant back to family to find him a wife so he won't take a wife from among the heathen in the land. Abraham's servant returns with the beautiful Rebecca as God's choice for Isaac, the miracle son of Sarah, and God's chosen heir of Abraham's covenant. With the help of his wife Rebecca, Isaac brings forth two sons, Esau and Jacob. Esau intermarries with the people of the land and becomes very spiritually dull, but Jacob stays separate by going to his uncle Laban's home. When Jacob and his sons end up in Egypt for 400 years, they live in the land of Goshen, separate and apart from the Egyptians! And when their descendants finally pass through the wilderness and come into the promised land, they are told not to intermarry with the people of the land or adopt any of their practices. Why is that? What is so bad about those pagans and their practices?

All the surrounding nations worshipped the Baals. Common to all Baal worship was, and is, sexual perversion. Baal was worshipped through temple prostitution and sexual orgies. The deities were viewed as beings to be alternately appeased or manipulated for human gain. (This tendency in us humans persists to this day!) The idea was that through orgiastic practices, the gods could be sexually excited to water the earth with their sperm to produce abundant crops. That is why Baal worshippers were often referred to as fertility cults. The gods were to be manipulated through extreme sexual sensuality to bring prosperity upon the earth. Of course, the allurement to this kind of unbridled sexual activity posed a very powerful temptation to the descendants of Abraham, Isaac, and Jacob.

God makes it clear that he wants the sexuality of his people surrendered to Him. So He calls Abraham and his descendants to make an exclusive covenant with him, as one does in a marriage.

When Abram was ninety-nine years old the Lord appeared to Abram and said to him, "I am God Almighty; walk before me, and be blameless, that I may make my covenant between me and you, and may multiply you greatly." Then Abram fell on his face. And God said to him, "Behold, my covenant is with you, and you shall be the father of a multitude of nations. No longer shall your name be called Abram, but your name shall be Abraham, for I have made you the father of a multitude of nations. I will make you exceedingly fruitful, and I will make you into nations, and kings shall come from you. And I will establish my covenant between me and you and your offspring after you throughout their generations for an everlasting covenant, to be God to you and to your offspring after you. And I will give to you and to your offspring after you the land of your sojournings, all the land of Canaan, for an everlasting possession, and I will be their God."

And God said to Abraham, "As for you, you shall keep my covenant, you and your offspring after you throughout their generations. *This is my covenant, which you shall keep, between me and you and your offspring after you: Every male among you shall be circumcised. You shall be circumcised in the flesh of your foreskins, and it shall be a sign of the covenant between me and you. He who is eight days old among you shall be circumcised. Every male throughout your generations, whether born in your house or bought with your money from any foreigner who is not of your offspring, both he who is born in your house and he who is bought with your money, shall surely be circumcised. So shall my covenant be in your flesh an everlasting covenant. Any uncircumcised male who is not circumcised in the flesh of his foreskin shall be cut off from his people; he has broken my covenant* (Genesis 17:1-14, ESV. Italics mine).

God wants a *wedding ring*. I say that somewhat facetiously, but as a sign of covenant faithfulness, God requires the *foreskin* from the organ of intimacy and knowing. Could there possibly be a clearer picture of God's desire for intimate relationship? "'They shall all *know* me, from the least of them to the greatest,' declares the LORD (Jer. 31:34)." Isn't that amazing! In a human marriage, we define faithfulness in sexual terms. God does too! That is why, especially in the Old Testament, idolatry and adultery are virtually synonymous and used interchangeably. To serve Baal, the God of sexual orgy, one had to be sexually unfaithful to God!

When we get into the period of the Kings of Israel, we meet Ahab and Jezebel. Jezebel is completely sold out to Baalism, and she leads God's people into the perversity of her pagan religion. One gets the idea from the lengthy narrative that Jezebel was energized by demonic power, and she used her sexuality to both manipulate and seduce. Ahab was a spineless puppet in her hands. She is such a strong symbol for the perversity of Baalism that her name appears in the Book of Revelation as a defiling spirit in the church.

Leanne Payne, founder of the School of Pastoral Care and a prolific author on issues of masculinity and the healing of the homosexual, says that we are currently experiencing *a resurgence of Baalism*, and she then gives numerous examples to back it up. I agree. We have become a sex-obsessed culture. Before the living God, we have an evil conscience, and we cower in fear and shame before our enemies, as Gideon did before the Midianites (Judges 6). If the men of the church are to regain their masculine soul, they must do as Gideon did and tear down the altars and Asherah poles (giant phallic symbols) to Baal. (See Leanne Payne, *The Healing Presence*, P. 196 ff.)

One of the most powerful dramas in the Bible, I Kings 18:20ff., is the contest between the prophet Elijah and Jezebel's four hundred fifty prophets of Baal. There are two altars, one built to sacrifice to Yahweh, the other to sacrifice to Baal. The challenge is for each to call upon their God to send down fire from heaven to consume the sacrifice. Before the contest begins, Elijah calls out to the crowd, "How long will you go limping between two opinions? If

Yahweh is God, then follow Him; but if Baal is God, follow him." Those words have been ringing continuously in my Spirit. I strongly sense they are a *now* Word. In that sense "there is nothing new under the sun." We are still fighting the same battle.

Elijah lets the prophets of Baal go first. They work themselves up into a frenzy to manipulate Baal to send fire. But nothing happens. Eventually they resort to self-mutilation with swords and lances until there's blood all over the place. But there's no response. Finally, Elijah rebuilds the altar to Yahweh, prepares the sacrifice, digs a trench around it, and then has it drenched in water three times. Then He calls upon the true and living God who sends fire from heaven that entirely consumes the burnt offering, the wood, the stones, the dust, and even the water. Finally, the people fall on their faces and cry, "Yahweh, he is God; Yahweh, He is God!"

All through the New Testament scriptures that exhort us to flee sexual impurity, I hear this same prophetic summons to stop limping between two opinions, to forsake Baal and worship the true and living God. The Lord seeks purity from His Bride, the Church. The purity of our corporate body and our personal bodies is so important to Him because our body is the temple of the Holy Spirit. We are His dwelling place, made in His image to reflect His glory.

I said this contest between Yahweh and Baal runs throughout the Scripture, and I meant that quite literally. In the very last book, the Revelation to John, we not only encounter the sexually immoral Jezebel (Rev. 2:20), but we meet the great harlot who rides on the head of the beast (Ch. 17). And finally, in the last two chapters at the end of the book, we see those who are excluded from the Tree of Life and suffer the second death: The cowards, the faithless, the murderers, the sexually immoral, sorcerers, idolaters, and all who love and practice falsehood.

But what about the beginning of the book, Genesis, the book of beginnings? Surely, there would not be any evidence of Baalism there. Or would there? This may sound strange, but I felt led to focus on the serpent in the story of the temptation and fall of mankind. I think most of us have come to accept the New Testament's interpretation of this Old Testament text that this talking serpent is a representation of the devil, the deceiver of the whole world. But why would he be represented as a *serpent*? I researched the word serpent and I discovered a number of interesting things. The oldest written language in the world is thought to be Sumerian, and the word for serpent in Sumerian is Ningizzida, which is actually a proper name, the name of a Sumerian fertility god! Furthermore, the serpent became the symbol for the pagan religions of Mesopotamia, Egypt, and Canaan.[29] So an ancient near eastern Jew might make the connection that the tempter would speak through the sexually-charged fertility cults of the surrounding nations! And whom do we meet at the end of the story, in the Book of Revelation? None other than that ancient serpent, the devil, whose sole desire is that we exchange the truth about God for a lie and worship and serve the creature rather than the Creator (Romans 1:25).

In the beginning, God created us in his own image, male and female. Man and woman together, in unity, reflect that image. And he tells man and woman to become one flesh, to be fruitful and multiply, and fill the earth. Anything that departs from the divine intention is a distortion of His will. And He is jealous over His creation, so jealous that He sacrifices the life of his first born son to bring it back to His intended purpose. He makes the god of this world an offer he can't refuse, blood redemption.

"You are not your own. You've been bought with a price. So glorify God in your body (I Cor. 6:19)."

There is a way out of all the sexual identity delusions because God has made a way through His Son, Messiah Jesus. He is the Way, the only way back to the Father and the knowledge of the True God, in whose image we are created. He is the Truth – which is the only word the Greek New Testament has for our modern term *reality*. To live in Jesus Christ is to live in reality, free from all delusion. And He is the Life, which is the beyond-time-and-space-consequence of intimately knowing and experiencing God (John 17:3).

It is axiomatic that none of us can know God apart from His self-revelation in Jesus. "No one has ever seen God; the only Son, who is in the bosom of the Father, he has made him known (John 1:18, RSV)." And Jesus Himself said, "Whoever has seen me has seen the Father (John 14:9, ESV)."

Furthermore, it is also axiomatic that none of us can know our own true identity apart from Jesus, the perfect expression of humanity. The apex of all healing ministry, all restoration, is to enter into full identification with Messiah Jesus in his circumcision, death, burial, resurrection, and ascension. In Romans 6:11, Paul says, " . . . consider yourselves dead to sin and alive to God *in Christ Jesus* (italics mine)." We can never know our true state by looking at our natural selves, but only by seeing ourselves *in Christ*.

This is the essence of the baptismal covenant into Christ: Being made one with Him. "If we have been *united with Him* in a death like His, we shall certainly be *united with Him* in a resurrection like His (Rom. 6:5). His death becomes my death. His burial becomes my burial. His resurrection becomes my resurrection. (Romans 6:3-5; Gal. 2:20; Col. 3:1) His circumcision becomes my circumcision, whether I am male or female (Col. 2:8-12). His ascension becomes my ascension (Eph. 1:15-2:7). Only in Him can we appropriate our true identity, including our sexual identity and proper role in his creative activity. As I indicated earlier, this is explained in fine detail in the companion *Handbook for Healing the Sexually Broken*.

There is a way out of the strong delusion and the coming wrath. His Name is Jesus, and He is the only reality there is.

BORN THAT WAY

The issue of gender confusion has become highly politically charged with oft-repeated slogans that people come to accept as truth, even when there is no evidence to support the truth of that slogan. Slogans, even if they are false, have a power to capture an entire society. Slogans often occur in a sentence that begins with "Everyone knows . . ." or "It is now generally accepted that . . ." or even more extreme "Science has now proven beyond reasonable doubt that . . ." People trained in logic recognize this persuasion technique as a logical fallacy. The constant repeating of a lie, a half truth, or even an unproven fact does not make something true. But truth is not the issue here. Truth is not even important in political issues. The only thing that matters is the *appearance* of truth, and the acceptance of the slogan as truth. If a large portion of society comes to accept the slogan as truth, their corporate faith takes on a nearly irresistible power, and power is the issue behind this political spirit.

This is the force that Jesus encountered when he was born into the Roman Empire where the crowds were compelled to worship the emperor as God and chant "Caesar is Lord!" The Jews resisted the tide of pagan society until Jesus came along and began to make claims about Himself that challenged the mental stronghold of the Roman Empire. Finally, when the pressure was on, the Jews caved to the pagan lie and passionately embraced it. Consequently, it cost Jesus His own life to challenge that commonly accepted lie of the emperor's divinity. The force of this politically correct mindset is revealed at the trial of Jesus before Pontius Pilate. When Jesus is presented by Pilate to the crowd as the King of the Jews, His own Jewish nation, with one voice, shouts the unthinkable: "We have no king but Caesar. Crucify him!"

One such logical fallacy in our society, which is gaining more and more credibility every day, has to do with acute gender identity confusion. How many times in the last couple of years have you heard prominent public figures, like Hillary Clinton [we might as well start at the top], assert as a scientifically established fact that people who self-identify as lesbians, homosexuals, bi-sexuals (and on and on) are *born that way*. People who have resisted the pressure of political correctness have a hard time dealing with this cherished belief that sexually confused people are *born that way* when they witness more and more people cave to the slogan and, either willingly or reluctantly, embrace it. Politically astute people, and no movement is more politically astute than the National Gay Task Force,[30] understand very few people are willing to stand against majority opinion, or what *appears to be* majority opinion. Remember, appearance is everything. Truth is not the issue.

It is time for some little kid in the crowd to stand up and say, "The emperor has no clothes!" It is time to push back against this slogan that the acutely gender confused are born that way. I have never believed, and do not now believe, that any form of homosexuality is genetically pre-determined. If you feel your defences rising, I encourage you and plead with you to lower your guard just long enough to see if I can offer a well-reasoned alternative to the current tidal wave of politically charged sloganeering.

First of all, there is no solid scientific evidence for a genetic link to alternative sexual behaviours. Although they search hard and long, and remain optimistic, honest scientists admit that no credible link is yet known. I will say more about the genetic issue later, because I am quite convinced that trail leads to nowhere.

Allow me to speak of my own experience as a counsellor. Four of the first men I counselled for acute gender identity confusion each volunteered, during the course of history-taking, that they remembered the exact day, time, and place when they made the conscious decision to embrace a homosexual identity. This is a decisive step beyond merely experiencing same-sex attraction. This is a choosing of an identity.

One was standing in a school yard during recess and he had just been harassed by some name-calling schoolmates. When they called him a "homo" (as they had many times before), he said, "I decided then and there, 'If that's who they say I am, that's what I'll be!' I remember it as clear as day. I remember the bitterness and the pain. I was in grade eight."

Another counselee had been struggling with the thoughts of being a homosexual for several months. After he graduated from high school, he got a job in the oil fields of northern Canada where all the employees stayed in trailers in a work camp. He said, "I was lying on my bed, staring at the ceiling and crying. I had just gotten off of work and it was late afternoon. I remember the sun was going down. It was quiet, and I was all alone. And I remember deciding that day that I must be a homosexual, so I wouldn't fight it anymore."

Still another said, "My parents already had four boys and they wanted a girl. As far back as I can remember, I knew that I was supposed to be a girl, so I tried to be that for my parents so they wouldn't be disappointed." I asked him how he knew and he said that his parents and brothers verbalized it all the time. I cite these examples from practical experience in counselling to say that the element of choice has always been apparent to me, even if it begins to take place at a pre-natal level, as is clearly explained in *The Secret Life of the Unborn Child* by Dr. Thomas Verny.

In the last 50 years, several studies have been done with homosexual men and their identical twin brothers to try to establish if homosexuality is a genetically inherited characteristic. Most of the studies concluded that a homosexual male will be somewhat more likely than a heterosexual male to have a brother who is also homosexual, but each of these studies said it was impossible to conclude that this tendency was strictly due to genetics, and not to the social environment which they shared. In short, there is no conclusive scientific evidence that homosexuality is a genetically inherited characteristic, no proof that people are *born that way.*

John and Paula Sandford of Elijah House Ministries have written several times over their 50+ years of ministry about their extensive experience in ministering healing to both male and female homosexuals. In the latest revision of the textbooks they authored to train prayer counsellors, they state " . . . the main reason why people become homosexuals is failure to identify with the same-sex parent. In today's society, many fathers no longer know how to be fathers, and mothers, increasingly, no longer know how to be mothers."[31] That leaves a child in a very vulnerable state. They go on to talk about how many such children then become the victims of rape or molestation and lack the inner resources to push back negative conclusions about themselves. Sexual abuse always assaults a person's sense of personhood to the very core, and de-stabilizes one's sense of well-being. This, in turn, makes a person extremely vulnerable to lies about one's personal identity. Depending on the extent and severity of the sexual abuse, very often the abuse is forgotten until there is a significant encounter with the Holy Spirit. Consequently, the sexual identity confusion seems to have no reasonable cause, and it is easy to conclude that the person was *born that way.*

Dr. Bruce Lipton, MD, PhD, cell biologist, pioneer in the new biology, and author of *The Biology of Belief,* was cloning stem cells in 1967! That's almost 50 years ago! You can't clone stem cells without a profound understanding of genetics. Dr. Lipton gives us some basic facts about our genes.

He says our genes:
- are only blueprints
- are neither "on" nor "off" as some currently teach
- are not "self-actualizing"
- are only read

- are read by the mind
- *can be altered – there are about 30,000 potential variations for the way each gene is expressed.*

Dr. Lipton asserts that the greatest influence on the expression of our DNA is our environment. He quotes Einstein on the debate about which is more dominant, particles or field. Einstein used metal filings to represent particles and magnetic force to demonstrate field. Metal filings placed on a table will fall into random patterns until a strong magnetic field is placed under the table. Then the filings will conform to the patterns in the magnetic field. In the same way, Lipton teaches, our environment is the field which influences the expression of our DNA.

By environment, he includes the field around us of mental and spiritual activity, commonly referred to as faith. Field is demonstrated in the placebo-based testing of prescription medications. Placebo based testing recognizes that people who believe a sugar pill can make them feel better or actually cure them, up to 40% of the time are actually cured, not because of the inert ingredients, but because of their faith![32] It is not uncommon for placebos to perform better in drug trials than the sophisticated drugs against which they are being tested. This is an embarrassing fact that is seldom shared with the general public, but is well-known in pharmaceutical laboratories.

Faith is at least one of the invisible forces that determines the way our genetic blueprint is expressed, thus the title of Lipton's award-winning book, *The Biology of Belief.* Newtonian physics, upon which conventional medicine is based, is mechanistic and doesn't understand this. Quantum physics, the new science, says it can be no other way! He says that our mind influences our biology, the conscious mind to some extent, but the subconscious mind to a much greater extent. Lipton says the subconscious mind is one million times more powerful than the conscious mind. That helps us to understand why mere cognitive therapy with acute gender confusion doesn't produce enduring results but spiritual therapy is much more successful.[33] Tragically, the people who make political decisions to ban "conversion therapy" or "reparative therapy" do so on the basis of extremely limited knowledge and under a lot of political pressure.

Our subconscious mind is programmed in the first six years of life. During that time, we uncritically download the behaviors, values, and beliefs of others, especially our parents. We are simply devouring experiences and information. We are in *record* mode. The subconscious then, runs all the programs in the background. We don't even have to think about them, and even if we try to think about them, we have a hard time over-riding them with the conscious mind. Try telling yourself "Don't panic" or "stop breathing" or "don't blink" or "don't laugh" or "don't cry" or "don't look now" or "don't be angry" or "don't be afraid" or "don't run" or "don't scream" or "stay awake". Those behaviors, sooner or later, will be determined by whatever is written on the hard drive, and can only be interrupted momentarily, which is why it is so important for the gay (political) movement to get their sex-ed curriculum into kindergarten and grade one to propagandize our children before they are six years old. King Solomon understood the battle for the minds of our children when he said, "Train up a child in the way he should go, and when he is old he will not depart from it (Proverbs 22:6, RSV)." In other words, write it on his hard drive – in more Hebrew terms *heart drive*! And if the heart drive has a bad program on it (For example, a boy might think, "My father raped me, therefore there is something wrong with me, I'm different, I was made to have sex with men" – or infinite variations of wrong conclusions about self), the heart drive needs to have new things written on it.

Most people tend to deal with some questions and insecurities about their sexuality that reach their crescendo in early to mid-adolescence. Now if that transitional period is compounded by doubts and questions arising from some level of sexual abuse in their childhood, the identity crisis is significantly intensified. The most conservative estimates say that 1 in 7 males and 1 in 4 females of the general population have been sexually abused in childhood. Estimates and national averages mean little in some neighbourhoods where it is difficult to find a child who has not been caught in the web of sexual abuse. The more intense and prolonged the sexual abuse has been, the more intense the sexual identity crisis, especially if the abuse has been forgotten by the conscious mind but held in the subconscious mind that runs the show.

Asserting that the acutely gender confused are *born that way* is meant to preclude any rational discussion of the causes of homosexuality. There are causes, as many causes as there are sexually-broken people, but it is important to recognize the universal and most basic cause of all human brokenness: SIN, and our consequent alienation from the very God who created us in His own image. I call that the primary cause, and it is common to all of us.

Because we are alienated from him, we are darkened in our understanding, and we become vulnerable to all the secondary causes. Secondary causes are variable and disputable, the primary cause is not! The atheist philosopher, Spinoza, at least had some notion of his own blindness when he said that we are all like "windowless monads" drifting in a dark universe! A brilliant description of man without God! And if we do not see and know the One who made us in His image, how can we possibly know the truth about ourselves and our identity? "Windowless monads" drifting in a dark universe can only say, "What is truth? All truth is relative. What is true for you may not be true for me. Only I can decide what is true for me." Some young people today choose a sexual identity like they choose a tattoo as an expression of uniqueness. I recently heard Lady Gaga, an iconic leader of this counter-culture, describe herself as *flexi-sexual.* It is foolish to under-estimate the influence and power of trend-setting figures like this to shape culture among our youth.

Once we establish sin and alienation from God as the *primary* cause of gender identity confusion, then we are able to look at all the secondary causes that all flow from the primary cause. This is where parents come in. The most important relationship we will ever have in this world is with our parents, simply because they are at the foundation of our being. Everything else is erected on the foundation.

The function of our earthly parents, who have a cooperative relationship with God in creating us, is to show us what God is like, to re-present Him.

- God is light, and in Him is no darkness at all.
- God is love, and this is how we know what love is, that Christ laid down his life for us.
- God is a community of three persons, Father, Son, and Holy Spirit, which is a mystery that can only be known and experienced by a fully-surrendered worshipping human spirit. He cannot be mastered with a mind that is inferior to the One who created it.
- Nothing and no one exists outside of God.
- As a Father, God provides everything for us, nurtures every need, protects us, and trains us to maturity to be His partners in governing his creation.
- Our creator God requires the totality of our being to be entirely yielded to Him in order that He might release the fullness of His love and blessing on us. It needs to be stated that the totality of our being includes our sexuality (witness the covenant of circumcision), our emotion and passion, our intellect, and all the wealth with which He entrusts us (i.e., the tithe is our acknowledgement that it all belongs to him, not to us).

In so far as our earthly parents (this includes all who stand in that role: birth parents, adoptive parents, foster parents, school teachers who function *in loco parentis,* police officers, mayors, priests, pastors, and presidents) – in so far as they fail to reveal God to us, to show us what God looks like with skin on, they have misrepresented Him and deprived us of what we need to know about our identity, our purpose, and the very meaning of our lives.

Now we are ready to spell out in more detail just a few of the more common secondary causes of acute gender identity confusion. These are the kinds of things people typically report to us as we hear their story:

- Little or no spiritual, emotional, mental, or physical bonding and attachment with the father or mother, or both, because of abandonment, spiritual slumber, emotional unavailability, terminal illness, death, workaholism, alcoholism, drug addiction, sexual addiction, and so forth.
- Gender rejection in the womb by mother or father, or both. They verbalize they want a boy when a girl is growing in the womb, or vice versa. That same gender rejection may continue on after birth, dressing a boy like a girl, or a girl like a boy, calling a boy by a girl's name, or a girl by a boy's name.
- Every kind of abuse (physical, mental, emotional, or sexual) erodes a sense of "self" and "well-being". We had a counsellee sexually abused in early childhood simultaneously by both her parents. As an adult she wore a pair of bib overalls and on the metal buttons was engraved the word *used*. I don't even know where you would buy clothes like that, but that was what was written on her heart drive before she was six years old. Of course she didn't remember it until she entered into some spiritual healing and got some new things written on her heart drive. She survived her horrendous childhood by developing a coping device called dissociative identity disorder. Only the power and presence of God in prayer ministry enabled her to begin facing the deeply repressed memories with forgiveness and faith.
- The next level is usually rejection and bullying from siblings and peers, especially if they sense weakness in a child's sense of personhood. Having been raised on the farm, I have witnessed cannibalism in chickens. They only

pick on those who are already bleeding. The same with kids. If there is a previous history of rejection from parents, the child has no resources (no truth base) to fight off the bullying words (hateful lies), which are usually ones used to try to pin a broken sexual identity on the child. If you've ever spent time in a schoolyard or on a school bus, you've heard it all: Faggot, queer, bitch, homo, lesbian, ugly, reject . . . and those are the nicer labels. I cannot help but believe that these bullying words and actions are demonically inspired. You can sense the demonic glee of the persecutors and the torment of the persecuted, even if they try to pretend that it doesn't bother them. Whether they want to or not, they are looking to their peers to tell them who they are. But those peers can be as cruel as cannibalistic chickens, picking their playmates into submission to a lying identity.

Recently, we heard in the media about the case of a California couple who took their 5 year old son in for a surgical sex change because he liked to dress like a girl. Consequently, they were hailed as heroes by those who reported in the press. What five year old makes that kind of choice for the rest of his life? And what kind of parents would rush him into it? That's what you would call *religious zeal!* This simply illustrates how this way of thinking is gaining such widespread social acceptance that the medical profession and the news media readily cooperate with it and promote it. That is the social environment in which we live today, and I contend that the environment itself is increasingly becoming a secondary cause of homosexuality. In 2 Corinthians 10:3-5, the apostle Paul says, "For though we walk in the flesh, we are not waging war according to the flesh. For the weapons of our warfare are not of the flesh but have divine power to destroy *strongholds*. We destroy *arguments* and every lofty *opinion* raised against the knowledge of God, and take every *thought* captive to obey Christ . . . (italics mine)"

I heard Argentinian evangelist, Ed Silvoso, founder of Harvest

Evangelism, offer a brilliant definition of a stronghold: "A stronghold is a mindset impregnated with hopelessness, which causes us to accept as unchangeable situations we know are contrary to the will of God." I believe that the perpetually repeated phrase, *born that way,* is a clear example of a mental stronghold that is gaining strength in western society.

A case in point: I know of a young man, a university student, who was struggling with his sexual identity. He made an appointment at the university to see a counsellor to discuss some relational conflicts he was having with a couple of male friends. She immediately had the answer for his problem. She told him he was obviously gay and needed to wholeheartedly accept and embrace his true identity to be at peace with himself and his male friends. From various reports I hear and read, this is becoming common practice in school counselling offices. I also know that the highly political gay movement is not only pushing for laws to forbid therapists to do reparative therapy – but to classify reparative therapy as a "hate crime." Some have become so militant that they will do anything to prevent those who actively seek and desire healing from same sex attraction from ever getting it. I cite this as yet another secondary cause of acute sexual identity confusion, meaning that an environment is being created to normalize homosexuality. It is an expressed political agenda.

My final answer to the belief that the lesbians and homosexuals are *born that way* is the overwhelming evidence of those who have found release from homosexual compulsions and fully self-identify as heterosexual men and women. There are a number of former homosexuals and lesbians who have written books or created videos available for viewing on You Tube to share their healing journey and ongoing freedom from homosexual compulsions. Many of these are included in the Bibliography. Some of these people are well-known, but many are not. Of course, the testimonies that are the most persuasive for me personally are the ones in which I had the privilege of being the counsellor and a primary member of the healing community. I participated in the battle, week to week. I labored in intercession. I struggled with my own doubts and fears about my own competence as a counsellor. I grieved over setbacks. I wept for joy when there were moments of breakthrough revelation. And I have celebrated abiding victories that have lasted now for 20 or 30 years.

Those who oppose what is called *reparative therapy* or *conversion therapy* often protest that the results are temporary and most revert to their previous gay lifestyle. That is a half-truth, and a half-truth is a lie. It is true that not all stay free. There are some, who for various reasons, go back to their former way of life. There is nothing new about that. Not all former alcoholics stay free. Not all former heroin addicts stay free. The brilliant actor and director, Philip Seymour Hoffman, was clean and sober for about twenty-three years, and then in a matter of a few short months, took a mighty fall that cost him his life.

It is well-known in the recovery community that secular-based programs have a *failure* rate in excess of 80%. Nevertheless, they persist because they have to try *something*. On the other hand, many spiritually-based programs have a *success* rate in excess of 80%. This is true for programs that deal with alcoholism, drug addiction, and sexual addictions. When David Wilkerson's Teen Challenge Organization began to demonstrate this kind of remarkable success with healing the addicted, they were invited to testify before the US Congress. The Congress wanted to know what accounted for the wide discrepancy in success rates between Teen Challenge and the secular humanist programs. The proceedings of that investigation came to be known as *The Jesus Factor.*[34]

I know that some people object to comparing recovery from sexual identity confusion with recovery from substance abuse and addiction, but the truth of the matter is that the path to freedom from any kind of human bondage has many factors in common: Confession, forgiveness, absolution, renunciation, renewal of the mind, healing community, training, and outreach to others who are still bound. All of these things are inherent in the gospel of the Lord Jesus Christ and his kingdom. To believe and to expect anything less is to hold that gospel in contempt.

At the risk of being repetitious, let me say it again: There is an important insight into the life of the early church in I Corinthians 6:9-11. There were many people in the early church who shared the sexual practices of our contemporaries who are supposedly *born that way.* "

"But you were washed!"
He means washed by the blood of Jesus,or washed in the waters of Baptism – either or both. But this also implies everything before and after the washing that there was confession of sin, and repentance – a turning away from these former things, and absolution – the pronouncement of complete forgiveness!

"You were sanctified!"
That means separated, set apart from your former way of life, which means that they went through a process of discipleship and healing of the inner man

"You were justified
...in the name of the Lord Jesus Christ and by the spirit of our God" means they were aligned with the purposes of God and then empowered by the Spirit of God to live the Christ life and carry on his ministry.

I have grown to love those 3 little verses!
"And such were some of you!" **Were!**

This is always the good news. "I was one of those! Was!
But look at me now! Washed, sanctified, justified.
TRANSFORMED!
I'm not the same person anymore.
I am a new creation in Christ.

The old has passed away!
The new has come!
I have been born again, from above (John 4).
I have been born anew to a living hope (I Peter 1:3).
And the same spirit that raised Jesus from the dead lives in me.
I'm here to set the captives free.
I'm here to show you the Way, the Truth, and the Life!
Follow me!"

The reality of the new birth and the new nature makes any talk about the old birth and the old nature irrelevant.

GAY IS NOT A GENDER

I frequently quote the newspaper columnist, Sydney Harris (1917-1986), who once wrote, "If we speak wrongly about something long enough, we will also think wrongly about it as well." After testing the maxim for years, I am convinced that it is consistently true.

A prime example is the use of the word *gay* as a term of self-identification as in: "Are you gay?" "Yes, I am gay."

So what does the word actually mean? In our society, I venture to say there is much confusion about the term. It appears to me that many, perhaps most people would equate the word *gay* with an entire spectrum of phenomena including, but not limited to:

1. All same-sex attracted people, either celibate or sexually active.

2. A male who copulates only with one other male.

3. A male who copulates with multiple males and females.

4. A male who self-identifies as female and has a surgical anatomical alteration.

4. A female who copulates only with one other female.

5. A female who copulates with multiple males and females.

6. A female who self-identifies as a male and has a surgical anatomical alteration.

I make that observation because the National Gay Task Force promotes and defends all of these alternative sexual behaviours that lie outside the purview of traditional marriage.[35] Furthermore, those who actively participate in gay pride parades and demonstrations, those who insinuate multiple sexualities into arts and the media, those who dominate the human rights tribunals, and those who wear down opponents of the gay agenda with expensive law suits in the courts, clearly intend to normalize each of these behaviours in our society.[36]

I think it is important to recognize that these are political organizations and political events with a political agenda: To normalize all sexual behaviour that deviates from the divine will of faithful monogamy between a man and a woman in the lifelong covenant of marriage.

To go back to the list above, there are many same-sex attracted people, celibate or sexually active, who do not identify themselves with the label *Gay*. They choose not to identify with the movement nor to become active in promoting the gay agenda. There are many same-sex attracted males and females who want freedom from those attractions and actively protest and resist when their friends, especially their "gay" friends, pressure them to accept the label. "Come out of the closet! Accept your true identity! Be proud of being gay! Join the movement!"

Gay is not a gender, it is identification with a political ideology and label. If a same sex attracted person accepts the label, they eventually take on the political agenda that comes with it, often without realizing it. Let me use an analogy to explain what I mean.

A number of years ago, I and a small group of young adults were having a lively conversation with a young man in our congregation who had strongly identified himself, even in his early teens, with a particular political party. He had come to our province from another province, and it just so happened that his political party was not very popular in our province. The other members of the group wanted to know why he would identify with this particular party, and then they began to challenge him in a good-natured way about a couple of planks in the political platform of his party, issues that were morally objectionable to the rest of the group. Although he seemed to be somewhat uncomfortable in doing so, I was surprised that he felt obligated to try to explain, defend and justify his party's positions on the controversial issues at hand. His words seemed to be at odds with his own moral inner-compass, as he strained to be loyal to the party he called his own. His generous friends essentially said to him in a kind way, "If that is what you have to believe and say to belong to that party, you can keep your party!"

I see a parallel dynamic at work in some same-sex attracted people who identify themselves as gay in that they are expected to take on the political agenda that goes with the label, even if they have some personal misgivings about it. Consequently, many of the same-sex attracted people I've spent time with oppose the political agenda and strongly object to being labeled by others as *gay*. They want freedom from their confusion and compulsions, and seek to distance themselves from the gay rights movement. In an article entitled "Why not say you're gay?" same-sex-attracted, but celibate, author Jonathan Berry says,

"I didn't like many of the associations that went with the gay label though, nor many of the assumptions that a lot of people back in the 80s would make about gay people, e.g. that you must be promiscuous, flamboyant, proud, at risk of becoming HIV+, etc."[37]

Berry goes on to say,

"The Bible knows nothing of the concept of 'sexual orientation' – so no one is ever referred to in the Bible as being gay, lesbian, straight, or bi-sexual. God's word speaks only of sexual practices, i.e., those which are pleasing to God (sex within marriage, which is between one man and one woman) and those which are not (all other sex, whatever the context). I now have a new identity, one which is based not on who I'm sexually attracted to, but rooted in my most important relationship of all, that is my relationship with Jesus Christ."[38]

So at the heart of this issue is where one locates their identity. Is it to be found in the changeable experience of one's sexual attractions and with a political cause that promotes and defends the unfettered expression of those attractions in all their forms? Or is that identity to be found in union with Jesus Christ and the redemptive cause of God's holy Kingdom?

"From now on, therefore, we regard no one according to the flesh. Even though we once regarded Christ according to the flesh, we regard him thus no longer. 17 Therefore, if anyone is in Christ, he is a new creation. The old has passed away; behold, the new has come (2 Corinthians 5:16-18 ESV)."

Words have creative power. Some words create reality. Other words create illusion. How can one know the difference? When Jesus says in John 14:6 "I am . . . the Truth (Greek: *he alethea*)," He is saying that He, the One through whom and for whom all things were made, is the complete embodiment of truth, which is the only word that Greek has to express the idea of *reality*. Jesus is the full expression of *reality!* Whatever conforms to the image of God's Son (Rom. 8:29) is real. And by contrast, anything that does not conform to His image is not real, but illusion.

It should be clear that there is a force in this world that is constantly seeking to create an alternative to reality, a convincing counterfeit that will turn men away from God and His Messiah, Jesus, who is the very image of the invisible God.

Many people have become convinced that gay, lesbian, bi-sexual, and other such images are a reality around which we must build a new society. My friend, Peter Fitch, claims to be "Actually Embracing People of Different Sexuality."[39] I refer to the public and politically-correct recognition of so-called different sexualities. When stating one's gender on Facebook, the choices are *male, female,* or *custom.* If one clicks *custom,* this opens a list of numerous options. ABC News Online counted 58 options in their report, but another website from the UK said their list ran to 71. I looked through both the American and British lists and could not find the term Lady Gaga has used to describe herself: *Flexisexual*. Concert crowds scream with delight to hear such imaginative words. Think of it! Another new human species has just created itself *ex nihilo!*[40]

This really is about creation. Do I submit to Another, revealed as the Creator, and allow Him to tell me who I am and why I'm here? Or do I claim to be the creator of my own identity because no one has the right to tell me who or what I am, and how I must live? I fully expect that from a world *alienated from the life of God, darkened in their understanding, and walking in the futility of their minds.*[41] But from those within the church? I'm speaking to the church, those who claim to be followers of Jesus. I'm speaking to the *Body of Christ, the physical manifestation of Jesus in the world today!*

True enough, political forces outside the church are gaining power and rising up, demanding that we as followers of Jesus conform our view of reality to that of the prevailing culture, which is by practice, being given over to a resurgence of ancient Baalism. And to be sure, there are growing consequences as these political forces increase in power and influence. Major corporations now threaten the livelihood of employees who do not conform to this new *enlightened* ethic. Independent business people are bankrupted by endless litigation if they do not conform to the new ethic. Small Christian Universities get blacklisted and are threatened with extinction if they do not conform to the new ethic.[42] But in the long view of history, there is nothing new about that. There is an Elijah versus Baal conflict for nearly every generation. The intensity of the conflict just seems new to those of us in the western world where the Church has had a compelling voice in our society for quite a few centuries.

One of the most clever things the National Gay Task Force has done was create the perception that gender identity and sexual conduct is purely and simply a civil rights issue, not an issue of creature accountability before the Creator of our beings in spirit, soul, and body. People who have fought for the civil rights of oppressed racial minorities, disenfranchised women, and oppressed children seem to have easily been persuaded that the gay agenda is the next great cause for human dignity and freedom. And so we see the Southern Poverty Law Center, founded in 1971 as a civil rights law firm, now taking its $250,000,000 war chest against anyone who disagrees with the gay agenda. On February 12, 2014, a New York Times columnist revealed their strategy. In essence, he said they intend to bankrupt Christian and Jewish organizations and individuals that dare to help people with same-sex attraction live lives consistent with their personal and religious principles.[43]

The confusion over civil rights versus moral accountability is intentional and exploited at every opportunity. Consequently, it appears that anyone who opposes the gay agenda as a civil rights issue appears to be fair game to be labelled as a bigot and a homophobe. These strategies are calculated to shame and intimidate any who oppose the agenda into agreement or the complicity of silence. It becomes difficult to maintain one's personal equilibrium, move forward in the cause of Christ, and avoid being drawn into skirmishes based on orchestrated delusion. But we must stay the course at all costs, loving the Lord our God with all our heart, and loving our neighbors – all our neighbors, even our political enemies – as ourselves.

If anyone imagines that this is only about "Live and let live," think again.

Gay is not a gender, it's a political agenda, highly charged with spiritual energy.

> Why do the nations conspire,
> and the peoples plot in vain?

The kings of the earth set themselves,
and the rulers take counsel together,
against the Lord and his anointed, saying,
"Let us burst their bonds asunder,
and cast their cords from us." – Ps. 2:1-3, NRSV

THE SCRIPTURES

The written Word of God
like the Incarnate Word of God
is both fully human and fully divine
And Life-and-Truth are found only
in the tension of this paradox.

For the past 24 years, in seeking to train people in the church for effective healing prayer ministry to those confused about their sexual identity, I have offered these observations to establish a foundation of truth:

We call homosexuality a lying identity because it doesn't line up with what exegetes commonly refer to as the *plain sense*[44] of the written Word of God:

1)   There is nothing in the Scriptures about the creation of homosexuals or alternate sexualities.
       2)   There are no prescriptions in the Scriptures for homosexual unions or any other sexual unions outside of a male-female marriage. They are clearly forbidden.
       3)   I Cor. 6 speaks of redemption from homosexual activity and all forms of sexual immorality, among other things, for those who are caught in it.

Ah yes, what about the written Word of God, also known as The Scriptures?
       A *plain sense* reading clearly creates some serious problems for those who wish to defend or promote same sex marriage within the church. Consequently, we are being offered new interpretations of the Scriptures that claim to invalidate our

traditional understanding of the ancient text.

Now I am not naive about biblical interpretation. Out of a passionate love for the truth, I have devoted most of my life to biblical interpretation. And a thorough study of the Scriptures has often led me to depart from the traditional understanding of my peers and speak out on more than one issue: Spiritual gifts, the Inclusion of Infants in the Lord's Supper as in the Passover, Inner Healing, the Resurrection of the Body, Women in Ministry, and a few others as well. More than once, I have paid a price for my unpopular-at-the-time convictions. Therefore, my past endeavors in biblical interpretation incline me to a natural sympathy for those who ask serious questions about biblical interpretation concerning matters of sexual identity and sexual behavior.

What concerns me the most is the very nature of our approach to the Scriptures in this current debate. It appears to me that we approach the Scriptures with an agenda, and then tailor an interpretation to fit that agenda. A *plain sense* reading of the Scriptures creates an apparent need to reinterpret them to accommodate the LGBT agenda. I know this is a risky business, but I can't help minding the warning in II Peter 3:16 where Peter says concerning the letters of Paul: "There are some things in them that are hard to understand, which the ignorant and unstable twist to their own destruction, as they do the other Scriptures (ESV)." Worthy of note is that some of the most disputed passages in the current debate about sexuality are in the letters of Paul! Now which of us would think we might be ignorant or unstable? Of course we think ourselves exempt and in no danger of twisting the Scriptures to our own destruction! Am I alone in suspecting a huge blindspot common to us all? I think we all need to exercise some holy caution here.

Has the church been wrong to call the Scriptures the sole rule and norm for faith and life? Perhaps, but what is the alternative? I'm sure *sole rule and norm* sounds a little rigid and hard to some folks, a definition lacking some spiritual vitality. A relic from days gone by. The sort of formula attractive to cold legalists. But I sense a significant degrading from that rather exclusive view of the Scriptures to one Peter Fitch articulates in his chapter, "What Is The Importance of the Bible?" He calls the Bible "an invaluable aid to Christian growth and maturing, a training ground, a trysting place, a source of wisdom, a traffic light, a directional sign and an icon."[45] He explains what he means by each of these poetic metaphors. To be sure, his words are warm and noble, and impossible to take issue with. Furthermore, they might apply to any great work of literature. I can think of scores of spiritual writings that are also worthy of these same appellations.

However – and this is a big *however* – the burning question of the hour concerns the intent of the *author* of all creation, who alone has the *authority* to determine the function of all that He has created. What has God said about this in the past, and what is He saying now? Has He expressed His will concerning the stewardship of our bodies (I Corinthians 6:19-20; Romans 12:1-2), and by extension, the stewardship of our material universe, including things like money, livestock, boundary makers, and weigh scales?

The followers of Jesus, the Incarnate Word of God, have traditionally looked to the Scriptures, the Written Word of God, for answers to those most fundamental questions of life. The current debate, however, is constantly being pushed into the realm of uncertainty by those who would rather keep God in an advisory capacity. "We can't know the will of the Creator because the Scriptures are unclear. And since the will of the Creator is not clear concerning the expression of human sexuality, it is up to us to decide. All we know for sure is that God is Love. Love is the fulfilling of all the law and the prophets, therefore anything we think that qualifies as love is consequently the will of God!" That is essentially the way that man-centered biblical interpretation (humanistic hermeneutics) works, and anyone can do it, and frankly, we all have the base inclination to do so! I have heard people who have been exposed and confronted for fornication, or adultery, or pedophilia, or polyamory do it in the context of pastoral care and church discipline to justify their actions: "But it was all done in love! How could that be wrong when it feels so right?" Truly, "there is nothing new under the sun!"

The justification of rebellion against the will of the Creator has to begin with challenging His Word. Genesis 3:1, "Did God say . . .?" "Uh, we don't know. We're not sure. There are eight passages in the Scriptures whose meanings are questionable, so it throws the whole issue into question . . ."

The reason I am so intent on asking this question about the very nature of the Scriptures is because of the way that Jesus, the Incarnate Word of God, aligns Himself with the Scriptures, the Written Word of God. At the inauguration of his ministry in Luke 4, he reads from the prophet Isaiah,

"The Spirit of the Lord is upon me,
   because he has anointed me
   to proclaim good news to the poor.
   He has sent me to proclaim liberty to the captives
   and recovery of sight to the blind,
   to set at liberty those who are oppressed,
   to proclaim the year of the Lord's favor."

Then he assumes the posture of authority by sitting down and[46] says,

"Today this Scripture has been fulfilled in your hearing (vv. 18-19, 21)."

Just prior to this event in the synagogue at Nazareth, Jesus had spent forty days in the wilderness being tempted by the devil. Three times Jesus overcame the delusions of the enemy with three words, "It is written . . ." Jesus fully submits to the authority of his Father, because those words essentially ring with the same meaning and authority as "Thus says the Lord . . ."

How many times did Jesus say to His opponents, "Have you never read . . .?" to make clear that what was happening in the present moment had already been revealed in the Scriptures to be the will of God?[47]

In John 5:39, we hear Jesus saying, "You search the Scriptures because you think that in them you have eternal life; and it is they that bear witness about me . . ." He didn't fault them for thinking they had eternal life in the Scriptures; he clearly agreed. But he did make it clear that in their reading of the Scriptures, they missed Him who is, in his very person, eternal life!

Jesus' deep identification with the sacred writings of the covenant people of God inspires me to treat them with a special reverence, a reverence that is apparently shared by the New Testament writers. According to Logos Bible Software, there are 355 occurrences in the New Testament of the expression "the Scriptures", often within this phrase: "in order that the Scriptures might be fulfilled." In most cases, "the Scriptures" are synonymous with "the definite plan and foreknowledge of God."[48]

There is also a passage in Hebrews 5:1-6 that speaks of how intimate is the relationship between the written Word of God and the Incarnate Word of God:

For every high priest chosen from among men is appointed to act on behalf of men in relation to God, to offer gifts and sacrifices for sins. He can deal gently with the ignorant and wayward, since he himself is beset with weakness. Because of this he is obligated to offer sacrifices for his own sins just as he does for those of the people. And no one takes this honor for himself, but only when called by God, just as Aaron was. So also Christ did not exalt himself to be made a high priest, but was appointed by him who said to him,

"You are my son,
today I have begotten you';

as he says also in another place,

"You are a priest forever,
            after the order of Melchizedek."

This, I think, is so very remarkable because Jesus' call and appointment from God comes through the words of Psalm 2. And there is no mistake that he is talking about the written word as the authoritative voice of God because of what it says right after that: "as he also says in another place . . ." What is clearly implied is *another place in the Scriptures.* God is speaking to Jesus, the Incarnate Word of God through the Scriptures, the Written Word of God.

The whole passage in Hebrews 5 is about the only one who has the authority to call and appoint someone to be a high priest: God alone. What is also clear is that God locates his authority in the Scriptures, the written Word. This is where He speaks,[49] and this is where Jesus hears Him! Does it not follow then, that anyone who earnestly desires to follow Jesus would seek to do the same?

Because the *plain sense* of Scripture poses so many difficulties for those who advocate or endorse same-sex marriage, we hear them cautioning us not to treat the Scriptures like a rulebook. I certainly understand the danger in that, and it's easy to see how such an approach has led to all kinds of peculiar practices and the forming of religious sects. It is obvious that many of us throughout history, in a zeal to obey God, have gotten some of the words right, but completely missed the intent of our wise, loving and merciful God. Our foolish misinterpretations are more a manifestation of the human brokenness that filters our understanding than an obvious need to adopt an antinomian view of the Scriptures to protect ourselves from error.

So, is the Bible a rulebook?

First off, the Bible isn't a book. It is a *compilation* of books written by a multitude of human authors over the period of at least a thousand years, and perhaps several thousand years. So it is really a book of books. All of those books taken together have been given a name, The Holy Bible, because we have recognized a common source in God, the author of creation. Furthermore, there is a recognition that the great book, the Holy Bible, has two parts that document a progressive relationship between God and the people He has made. The English terms to describe those parts are somewhat misleading, the Old Testament and the New Testament. The Greek terms are Old Covenant and New Covenant (diatheke). Covenant is the ancient word that permeates the Bible itself, and helps us to address the question.

God chose to reveal Himself and His desired relationship to mankind through the near eastern cultural forms of covenant, particularly a suzerain-vassal covenant. The suzerain was one possessing vast wealth and power. The vassal was one in need of the basics of survival, namely provision and protection. Thus, the relationship was often defined in Father-Son language, or Lord-Servant terms.

The suzerain-vassal style covenant, as we see that God makes with Adam, then Noah, then Abram, then Moses, then David traditionally follows a form that includes some or all of these parts:

The Preamble
The historical Prologue
The Stipulations
The Blessings
The Curses
The Witnesses
The Place of Deposit
The Periodic Reading

For example:

The Preamble - "I, Yahweh, your God . . ."

The historical Prologue - " . . . who brought you out of Egypt . . ."

The Stipulations - Commandments, Statutes, and ordinances

The Blessings - A land, a name, a people if you obey my voice

The Curses - Lose all if you do not obey my voice

The Witnesses - God swears by Himself

The Place of Deposit - Ark of the Covenant, Tabernacle, Temple

The Periodic Reading - Appointed Feasts

The Bible, that is the written Word of God, is a covenant that comes to us in two installments, if you will, referred to as the Old Covenant and the New Covenant. The Old Covenant, rather than being done away with, is comprehended in the New Covenant. As Jesus says in Matthew 5:17, "Do not think that I have come to abolish the law or the prophets . . . but to fulfill them."

There are stipulations in both covenants, as there are in any suzerain-vassal covenant. The powerful one, in this case, God, spells out the terms of the relationship. We might call those stipulations the commandments, or "rules."

The Scriptures are replete with synonyms to describe these various expressions of the will of God: Commandments, ordinances, precepts, testimonies, statutes, rules, your word, your law. This is especially true of Psalm 119, the longest Psalm in the Bible, which essentially speaks of nothing else!

Oh, how I love your law!
    It is my meditation all the day.
    Your commandment makes me wiser than my enemies,
    for it is ever with me.
    I have more understanding than all my teachers,
    for your testimonies are my meditation.
    I understand more than the aged,
    for I keep your precepts.
    I hold back my feet from every evil way,
    in order to keep your word.
    I do not turn aside from your rules,
    for you have taught me.

How sweet are your words to my taste,
sweeter than honey to my mouth!
Through your precepts I get understanding;
therefore I hate every false way (Psalm 119:97-104).

The Bible is not, in itself, a rulebook. Rather, it is a covenant in two parts. But the covenant includes chapters (such as Matthew 5 - 7) and large portions of books devoted to the rules, the law, the stipulations, whatever you want to call them in order to make clear the will of the God who has created us for His own pleasure and glory. A covenant is an eternal love relationship, because that is God's very nature. God is love. He takes us up into Himself, absorbs us into His own love community of Father, Son, and Holy Spirit. Nevertheless, He does not divorce His love from His will. He says, "If you love me, you will keep my commandments."

This is not legalism. Legalism means that one believes we can be saved and are saved by keeping the law, that is, the will of God, perfectly and in every aspect. Only Jesus did that, and we are saved by our faith in Him, His perfect obedience, and his perfect blood sacrifice that pays our penalty and delivers us from death. Nevertheless, our obedience, no matter how unpopular the subject these days, matters to God. Take note of the fact that the Apostle Paul both begins and ends his letter to the Romans (1:5; 16:26) – that great exposition on the grace of God – by announcing that his mission is "to bring about the *obedience of faith.*" Obedience now stands on a different foundation, to be sure, but it also has new respondents, new creatures in Christ who are filled with the empowering presence of God. "It is no longer I who live, but Christ who lives in me (Gal. 2:20)!"

We do not need to diminish the authority of God or His Word to find our way out of this difficult dilemma that threatens to splinter the church once again. But we do need to learn to live with some tension for awhile and not bite and devour one another until we do. I believe this requires a deep, mutual submission to the only One who truly knows the way.

All praise, honor, glory, and dominion be to Him who sits upon the throne, and to the Lamb, forever and ever!

Marriage

The scriptures begin with these words: "In the beginning, **God** . . ."

In a sense, the Scriptures are only about Him. Everything is "to him, and through him, and for him." He is the beginning and the end, and nothing exists apart from him. All that exists arises from him, and is an expression and extension of his being.

"In the beginning, God **created** . . ." Clearly, he has complete authority over all that exists, for he is the author. What he created, he created for himself and for his own pleasure. At each successive stage of calling things into existence, the text says that God saw that it was good. Good is a relative word, and in this case, relative to the Divine intention. Nothing went amiss. It came forth as He intended.

In this current discussion about same-sex marriage, what often seems to be missing is any talk about the Divine intention. It seems to revolve so much around what people think and desire, but those human thoughts and desires need to be evaluated in the light of the creator's intentions.

The creator of all things does have a clear intention for his creation. I think it's the same way when we humans create things. I have many vivid memories of my children when they were young and practising their creative skills. If we were by the ocean, and one child began making sand castles, there was always a rising of tension if one of the other children came along and wanted to make changes or improvements. We would hear this loud, painful, "No!" and we knew a rapid intervention was necessary! The first child already had a plan, a picture in the imagination of how things should be. As parents, we had to make a quick decision. Would it be possible to have the first child share the creative vision, so that the second child could join him in the creative endeavor? Or was it necessary to divide the beach, and set boundaries around each child, so that each could enter into parallel play and create their dream without interference?

It's not really my intention to compare the creator of the world with an immature child, but most human beings are the most creative when they are children, and then give up that creativity as they get older. But let the point come home. The Genesis account reveals the divine intent, and it is our responsibility, our obligation, as his created beings to fully comprehend and submit to that divine intent.

What is clear, at least to most students of the Word, is the contrast between chaos and order in the Genesis narrative. The creator of all things, as a potter with a lump of clay, imposes his order on his creation. And what is remarkable about this order is the tension between dissimilar, or even opposing things which work together to create a dynamic, powerful whole. Light and darkness together make a whole day. Water and dry land together make a whole planet. And so on.

Finally, as the crowning act of his creation, God fashions a human being in his own image, his own likeness, but the male alone is insufficient to adequately reflect the full creative glory of God. So God brings forth another human being who is both similar and dissimilar, and the male is given a female partner to complete him. The intent is that male and female together will reflect the image of the One who made them. They are given a creative role to play: "be fruitful and multiply and fill the earth . . . (Genesis 1:28)."

Furthermore, the Divine intention anticipates a process that extends to the end of time. "Therefore a man shall leave his father and his mother and hold fast to his wife, and they shall become one flesh (Genesis 2:24)." The durability of this prescription for a one flesh union is attested by the fact that this particular verse is quoted thousands of years later by Jesus himself in Matthew 19:5 and Mark 10:7, and then by the apostle Paul in I Corinthians 6:16 and Ephesians 5:31.

The conversation in the parallel accounts of Matthew 19 and Mark 10 concerns the destruction of the one flesh union through divorce. The Pharisees want to know if Jesus will contradict Moses, who allowed a man to divorce his wife. Jesus acknowledges the fact that Moses allowed a man to dissolve the covenant union of marriage and send his wife away. But he doesn't leave it at that. He goes on to say that Moses only did that "because of your hardness of heart." Notice he doesn't say *their* hardness of heart, referring to the men who lived in the days of Moses. He brings it home and makes it personal to the people who are asking the question, because the only reason they're asking this question is because they have the same problem, hardness of heart, for which they want justification. This is a continuous, ongoing departure from the will of God. It is because of *your* hardness of heart.

But here is the telling line: "but from the beginning *of creation* (compare Matthew 19:8 with Mark 10:6) it was not so." Any Mosaic concessions to human unfaithfulness are held up to the light of the divine intention at the foundation of the world. Many proponents of same sex marriage like to point to examples from the Scriptures of significant departures from a monogamous male-female one flesh union, for example, the polygamous patriarchs, Abraham, Isaac, and Jacob, and the two greatest kings of Israel, David and Solomon. This is meant to imply that the issue is a minor one and that God doesn't really care that much. Might I point out that the biblical narrative is primarily descriptive, not prescriptive. Why would I say that? There are people, even in the church today, who try to use these scriptures to justify and even promote wife-swapping, which now has the more euphemistic title, "polyamory" or "open marriage," all of course in the name of "love."[50]

In the midst of this whole tide of covenant-breaking, Yahweh-in-the-Flesh stands within our human story and points us back to His original plan, His divine intention: "From the beginning of creation, it was not so." In other words, "I haven't changed My mind." He keeps pointing us back to the book of beginnings, and asking, "*Have you not read* that he who created them from the beginning made them *male and female,* and said, Therefore a man shall leave his father and his mother and hold fast to his wife, and *the two shall become one flesh.* So they are no longer two but one flesh. What therefore God has joined together, let not man separate (*emphasis mine*)." According to the divine intent, the one flesh union is a union of male and female, and one that is capable, like everything else in the order of creation, of continuing the creation process, of producing offspring, each after its own kind.

In an article entitled "What's wrong with a permanent, faithful, stable same-sex relationship?" by Ed Shaw of LivingOut.org, there is a sub-section entitled "Real Sex is unity in difference." (What I love about this website is that it is hosted by people who are, or have been same-sex attracted, but who adhere to the divine intent. Celibacy is an acceptable alternative to traditional marriage for them.)

Allow me to quote Ed, who then quotes a woman who lived in a same-sex relationship for several years. It is, I think, one of the most brilliant insights I've ever read into the true nature of a one flesh union between a male and a female, and why the difference between male and female is so important.

So actually what often makes heterosexual sexual relationships so difficult for humans – the difference between the sexes – is what makes them so beautiful in God's sight. Melinda Selmys, a

Christian, with experience of both heterosexual and homosexual relationships, reflects on this:

"It is because of, and not in spite of, the tensions between the sexes that marriage works. Masculinity and femininity each have their vices and their strengths. The difficulty when you have two women or two men together is that they understand each other too well, and are thus inclined more to excuse than forgive. That frank bafflement which inevitably sets in, in any heterosexual relationship ("Why on earth would he do that? I just don't understand . . .") never set in throughout all the years that my girlfriend and I were together-naturally enough. We were both women, and we chose each other because we seemed to be particularly compatible women."

Males and females are not the same, but are uniquely different in a multitude of ways. Furthermore, children need both a male and the female parent, and if that is not possible, a prominent male or female parental figure. This is an issue that needs to be taken seriously by the church today to nurture and embrace our many single-parent families. In the purest sense, these are the modern-day widows and orphans, and as the Scriptures say, "God sets the solitary in families (Psalm 68:6, NKJV)."

All of the social decisions that we are making today on behalf of same-sex attracted people need to be made in the light of the divine intent. It is true that those who fear the Lord cannot dictate to a secular society a biblical morality that is disconnected from an experience with the living God. However, we do need to speak against a political tide that is determined to silence the biblical witness and to shackle the ministry of the church.

We need to acknowledge the fact that the church of the past has spoken against homosexuality without compassion and with very little understanding. We have a serious responsibility to gain understanding, and to gain it quickly. There is no acceptable excuse for our ignorance. And when we gain understanding, I am confident we will grow in our compassion.

We're standing at the crossroads at the moment. I know, based on the experience of 35 years of counselling ministry, that there is deep and abiding healing for unwanted same-sex attraction, which I prefer to call acute sexual identity confusion. And I also know, that if we don't embrace the healing ministry of Jesus in this dimension of the church's life, we will eventually have to capitulate to the ways of the unbelieving world and share both their unbelief and their contempt for the good news of complete healing in the Lord Jesus Christ.

I am currently in the process of following up this work with a handbook for ministering to the sexually broken, but there are already several excellent resources available which are listed in the bibliography.

Allow me to quote again from Leanne Payne of blessed memory, the opening words of her little book, *Healing Homosexuality:*
    "As a sexual neurosis, homosexuality is regarded as one of the most complex. As a condition for God to heal, it is (in spite of widespread belief to the contrary) remarkably simple."

Let us do the remarkably simple.

ENDNOTES

[1] Rich Nathan, in his essay on "Understanding and Responding to the Recent Supreme Court Decision on Gay Marriage," July 10, 2015, says this about the prevailing worldview in western society: " . . . this Supreme Court decision regarding same-sex marriage is, in my opinion, just another manifestation of the most deeply held philosophy in America today. That philosophy was termed **"expressive individualism"** by the famous Berkeley University sociologist, Robert Bellah, back in 1990. Expressive individualism basically holds that the supreme value to which every other obligation must be subordinated is the **true self within.** We

communicate expressive individualism by sound bites such as "it just feels natural to me." Or "I need to be true to myself." Or "I'm not going to live a lie."

2 Peter Fitch, *Learning to Interpret TOWARD LOVE, Pp. 8-9.*

3 I preached a message on "Women in Ministry" at the Toronto Airport Vineyard Christian Fellowship (now known as Catch The Fire Toronto) in September 1995 that literally went around the world via cassette and video tape. I was also asked to write a feature article on the same issue in December 1997 for their magazine and from which I received comments and criticisms up until 2014.   The article is a greatly condensed version of that original message and can be found here: http://revivalmag.com/article/truth-about-women-public-ministry My wife and I were also interviewed on national television about that subject http://100huntley.com/video.php?id=uWhCVhMPTVY

4 Don Rousu, *Handbook for Healing the Sexually Broken.* Unpublished at this writing.

5 For more insight on this, I recommend Peter Scazzero's excellent book, *The Emotionally Healthy Church.* Grand Rapids: Zondervan, 2003, revised 2010.

6 See the Family Watch International documentary, "Understanding Same-sex Attraction," https://www.youtube.com/watch?v=jJhyzqdzpnM

7 Matthew 17:14-21; Mark 9:14-29. Although the two responses differ, there is no doubt a relationship between little faith and a lack of prayer (and fasting).

8 http://www.christianitytoday.com/gleanings/2013/june/alan-chambers-apologizes-to-gay-community-exodus.html

9 The companion to this work, *Handbook for Healing the Sexually Broken* by Don Rousu, contains the Solomon material on appropriating our true identity in Christ. As well, Solomon's book, *Handbook To Happiness,* is included in the bibliography.

10 Rousu, op. cit.

11 For the record, I have spoken out, as an invited guest speaker, in a large public forum in a congregation of the United Church in Canada against the ordination of practicing homosexuals for ministry in the church. In that same forum, I also strongly

advocated the ordination to public ministry of those who have been *healed* of their homosexual identity and behaviors, of whom there are many.

[12] These terms are all thoroughly explained in the companion *Handbook for Healing the Sexually Broken.*

[13] John Eldredge, *Waking The Dead,* p. *13.*

[14] Please don't misunderstand me! I'm not advocating that we do this today. Nor am I certain that they actually carried it out in the days of Moses, Joshua, the Judges, or the Kings. The only thing I wish to highlight is the severity of the consequences.

[15] Theodore G. Tappert, translator and editor, *The Book of Concord,* St. Louis: Concordia Publishing House, Luther's Large Catechism, The Fourth Commandment, p. 379, paragraph 106

[16] From a course by Dr. Robert Bertram, "The Biblical Message and the World Today," Concordia Seminary St. Louis, Missouri, 1968. This is the force of the phrase "a little leaven leavens the whole lump." The sin of the individual defiles the whole body and makes it liable for judgment. The Corinthians were tolerating the sin and even boasting about it. I'm wondering if we're not proposing to do the same thing today in the name of "love."

[17] This will be dealt with in much more detail later.

[18] Scot McKnight http://www.patheos.com/blogs/jesuscreed/ 2015/04/06/did-jesus-talk-about-homosexuality/

[19] Matthew 11:11-14 - "Truly, I say to you, among those born of women there has arisen no one greater than John the Baptist. Yet the one who is least in the kingdom of heaven is greater than he. 12 From the days of John the Baptist until now the kingdom of heaven has suffered violence, and the violent take it by force. 13 For all the Prophets and the Law prophesied until John, 14 *and if you are willing to accept it, he is Elijah who is to come." (ESV, Emphasis mine).*

[20] McKnight, op cit.

[21] Oepke, anhr in the NT, *Theological Dictionary of the New Testament,* ed. by Gerhard Kittel, translated by Geoffrey W. Bromiley, p. 362.

[22] To demonstrate just how profound this conversion was, I am citing this priceless quote:

What Is A Christian?

At the beginning of the second century, Christians were described by the Athenian orator, Aristides, thusly:

"The Christians know God and trust in Him. They forgive those who oppress them, and make them their friends. They are good to their enemies. Their wives keep marriage pure; their daughters are chaste. They love one another. They do not refuse to help widows. When they see a stranger, they receive him in their house And rejoice at him as at a brother. If any among them is poor or in need, they fast for two or three days in order to satisfy his needs. They obey conscientiously the commandments their Messiah has given them. Every morning and every hour, they praise God and thank Him for His goodness. They are the source of all that is beautiful in the world. They do not speak publicly of their good deeds, but take good care not to be observed by any man. They are in truth a new people, and there is something divine in them."
- from *Christ on the Jewish Road* by Richard Wurmbrand

[23] Peter Fitch, op cit, *P. 59*

[24] Fitch, op cit. P. 62

[25] Fitch, op cit, P. 63

[26] For a more extended version of this summary document, see *The Overhauling of Straight America* by Marshall Kirk and Erastes Pill. http://library.gayhomeland.org/0018/EN/EN_Overhauling_Straight.htm

[27] Ben Brody, http://www.bloomberg.com/politics/articles/2015-05-22/americans-vastly-overestimate-size-of-lgbt-population

[28] Colin Cook, from an interview in Ministry Magazine, September, 1981, entitled "Homosexual Healing", P. 10. The entire issue can be downloaded at https://www.ministrymagazine.org/archives/1981/MIN1981-09.pdf

[29] Serpent (Bible), Wikipedia. Article last modified 26 September 2013

[30] 30.Peruse their website http://www.thetaskforce.org/ to see what I mean about political astuteness.

[31] Sandford, John Loren and Paula, *Letting Go of Your Past,* P. 150

[32] 32.From a video interview with Dr. Bruce Lipton https://

www.youtube.com/watch?v=wooTroHsiyk

[33] 33.So-called "conversion therapy" or "reparative therapy" has come under sharp criticism lately to the point that President Obama wants to be see it outlawed. In Canada, as of June 2015, the province of Ontario has already banned "conversion therapy" for children under the age of 18 and Manitoba is, at this writing, considering passing a similar law. This approach, operating on the assumptions of secular humanism, belongs to the genre of cognitive therapy. But there are people making vast strides with more spiritual approaches that get beyond the conscious mind to the underlying beliefs that populate the subconscious. I refer to people like Dr. Alex Loyd, author of *The Healing Code* (co-authored by Dr. Ben Johnson) and *Beyond Willpower;* Larry Napier, author of *Releasing the LION, Rediscovering the Right Brain HEART;* Dr. Ed Smith, developer of Theophostic Prayer Ministry; Dr. Karl Lehman, developer of *The Immanuel Approach;* and Dr. James Wilder, Ed Khouri, Chris Coursey, and Sheila Sutton, *Joy Starts Here, the Transformation Zone,* to mention just a few.

[34] 34.Association of Christian Alcohol and Drug Counselors Institute, "Significant Research That Everyone Should Know," http://www.acadc.org/page/page/2495014.htm

[35] http://www.thetaskforce.org/ Home page

[36] One outstanding example is the Southern Poverty Law Center, http://www.splcenter.org/

[37] Article posted on LivingOut.org, a website that represents a large number of same-sex attracted people, all Christians and many of them church professionals, who strongly advocate traditional marriage and celibacy for the unmarried.

[38] Berry, LivingOut.org, op cit.

[39] Fitch, op cit. front cover, book subtitle

[40] A play on a commonly held Christian doctrine that God created the universe out of nothing, from the Latin, *creatio ex nihilo.*

[41] All phrases from Ephesians 4:17,18.

[42] Concurrent to this writing, the Government of British Columbia, under pressure from the B.C. Law Society, has withdrawn support for Trinity Western University in Langley, B.C. to open a school of

law in 2016 because the students at that institution voluntarily submit to a policy to abstain from sex outside the marriage of a man and a woman. Other provincial governments are now supporting this decision by the B.C. government as they come under the political pressure of the law societies within their own provinces.

In all fairness, Christian Schools or Organizations that begin to deviate from strict policies of excluding same-sex attracted people from positions of employment are also threatened by their constituencies with the withdrawal of financial support and extinction. Such was the case in 2015 when, for one day, World Vision's Board of Directors announced their intention to employ same-sex attracted people as office staff. The consequent reaction from their supporters quickly persuaded them to reverse that decision the next day.

[43] From a fund-raising letter by trial lawyer Charles LiMandri of Freedom of Conscience Defense Fund, dated February 19, 2014. The NYT article which he cites is dated February 12, 2014.

[44] I understand the risk of being marginalized as a literalist by using this term, but what I mean by a *plain sense* reading of the text is what remains after we have eliminated, in so far as we are able, the possibilities of taking a text out of its historical context; eliminated the possibilities of irony, word play, metaphor, or multi-level symbols of communication; eliminated the possibilities, in so far as we are able, of imposing our own emotional, cultural, or religious bias on the text. Not everything in scripture is buried under layers of complexity. If all of the creation narratives speak only of male and female people, I take that to be a simple and uncomplicated observation. What we make of that might be another matter.

[45] Fitch, op cit, P. 123

[46] In Judaic tradition, we stand to read and we sit to teach. The understanding that the seated position is one of authority is reflected throughout history with the Latin expression, *ex cathedra,* literally "from the chair" or "from the throne." When a sovereign ruler makes a pronouncement that is binding on all the

subjects, he (she) does it *ex cathedra*. The same holds true in the papacy of the Roman Catholic Church. Several world governments, including Great Britain and Canada, also have speeches "from the throne" where the speaker is conspicuously seated.

[47] Three that immediately come to mind are Matthew 21:16; Matthew 21:42, and Mark 2:25.

[48] As in Acts 2:23

[49] Note: I am neither saying nor implying that God speaks *exclusively* through the Scriptures. The Scriptures themselves defeat that notion as when recounting the incident of the burning bush, the voice from heaven at the baptism of Jesus, etc. However, within the context of this discussion, we wish to acknowledge the authority that Jesus Himself gives to the written Word.

[50] The purest form of love, from a biblical perspective is *agape* love, which is an attribute of God, an ability which He pours into our hearts through the Holy Spirit, according to Romans 5:3-5. The nature of *Agape* love is manifest in Jesus laying down his life for us, I John 3:16. What the world calls "love" primarily speaks of human attraction or desire, which is acquisitive rather than sacrificial. The whole discussion about same-sex attraction tends to use this narrow definition of love, which is derived from the Greek noun, *eros* (English cognates: erotic, eroticism - to arouse desire). *Eros* is best understood as infatuation. There is nothing wrong or evil about *eros* love. The Song of Solomon celebrates it as we read about a young man making love to his wife on their wedding night. But *eros*, apart from *philia* (friendship love) and *agape* (sacrificial love) is fleeting and altogether insufficient upon which to build an enduring relationship. We can fall out of that kind of love as easily as we fall into it. Because enduring marital and familial relationships (Greek: *storge* love) are the bedrock of a stable society, we need to speak with clarity about the meaning of love and not be easily swayed in our societal decisions on the basis of "love."

BIBLIOGRAPHY

Allberry, Sam; Doherty, Sean; Shaw, Ed. *LivingOut.org. A biblical perspective on being Christian and gay*, continuously updated website.

Butterfield, Rosaria Champagne. *My Train Wreck Conversion.* Christianity Today January/February, 2013.

Comiskey, Andrew. *Pursuing Sexual Wholeness, How Jesus Heals the Homosexual.* Lake Mary: Creation House, 1989.

Di Sabatino, David. *FRISBEE, The Life and Death of a Hippie Preacher,* video documentary. Los Angeles: Jester Media, 2006.

Fitch, Peter. *Learning to Interpret TOWARD LOVE.* St. Stephen: The-volution Press, 2013.

Lee, Justin. *Torn: Rescuing the Gospel from the Gay vs. Christian Debate.* New York: Jericho Books, 2012.

Lipton, Bruce. *The Biology of Belief.* Carlsbad: Hay House, Inc., Revised 2008.

Loyd, Alexander; Johnson, Ben. *The Healing Code.* New York: Grand Central Life & Style, 2010.

Loyd, Alexander. *Beyond Willpower.* New York: Harmony Books, 2015.

Oostrum, Richard. *A Guy Who Was Gay.* Lottbridge Drove: Kingsway Communications Ltd, 2006.

Payne, Leanne. *Healing Homosexuality.* Grand Rapids: Hamewith Books, 1985.

Payne, Leanne. *The Broken Image: Restoring Personal Wholeness Through Healing Prayer.* Westchester: Crossway Books, 1981.

Payne, Leanne. *The Healing Presence.* Westchester: Crossway Books, 1989.

Rousu, Don and Ruth. *Healing and Mentoring the Inner Man" aka Prayer Counselling Course.* http://sites.radiantwebtools.com/?i=3081&mid=12, last revision 2007.

Sandford, John & Mark. *Deliverance and Inner Healing.* Grand Rapids: Fleming H. Revell, 1992.

Sandford, John & Paula. *Healing The Wounded Spirit.* South Plainfield: Logos, 1985.

Sandford, John & Paula. *Letting Go of Your Past.* Lake Mary: Charisma House Book Group, 2008.

Sandford, John & Paula. *Restoring The Christian Family.* Tulsa: Victory House, Inc., 1979.

Sandford, John & Paula. *Transformation of the Inner Man.* South Plainfield: Logos, 1982.

Sandford, John. *Why Some Christians Commit Adultery.* Tulsa: Victory House, Inc., 1989.

Solomon, Dr. Charles R. *Handbook to Happiness, A Biblical Guide to Victorious Living.* Carol Stream: Tyndale House Publishers, Inc., 1971, 1989, 1999.

Vineyard USA Executive Team on behalf of Vineyard USA.

Pastoring LGBT Persons, Position Paper, 2014.

Wilder, E. James; Khouri, Edward; Coursey, Chris; Sutton, Sheila. *JOY Starts Here, the transformation zone.* East Peoria: Shepherd's House, 2013.

Wilson, Ken; Gushee, David P.; Tickle, Phyllis; Luhrmann, T. M. *A Letter to My Congregation.* Kindle Edition, 2014.

ACKNOWLEDGMENTS

Writing a book is truly a community project. I want to express my thanks for all those who gave of their precious time to read this manuscript, in whole or in part, to weed out the technical errors and also to critique my thoughts and the way they were expressed: Nathan and Charis Rousu, Ed Hilchey, Terry Harsch, Larry Levy, Brian Metzger, Derek Morphew, Katherine Walden, Art and Cyndi Rae, Deanna Rode, and Joe Kelder. There were many others who read it without submitting critical comments, but only offered words of encouragement to not quit until it was in print! Thank you all so much. You had a big hand in this project.

Any writing project requires willing sacrifice from immediate family as we set aside family holidays and special together times to see something like this to completion. My dear wife, Ruth, has been totally onboard with the writing of this book, having fully participated in the healing ministry that brought it about. Well, sweetheart, it's done. Let's go play for awhile!

Finally, I owe a tremendous debt of gratitude to Katherine Walden, a member of our church and a published author (*Seasons* and *Dare to Call Him Friend*) who offered to get this thing formatted and off to the press. It is one thing to write a book. It is quite another to publish one. I frankly felt quite overwhelmed and intimidated with trying to learn all the new skills required for this last step in the midst of all my other work responsibilities. I feel as though I've been given a hand and lifted out of the pit! Thank you for rescuing me – and this book, and for believing that it needed to be widely read.

And it was Katherine who led me to Alice Briggs who has designed the cover for this book. Thank you, Alice, for your creative gift. They say in Africa, "It takes a village to raise a child" and I think it also takes a small village to write a book. That is both humbling and gratifying. I am blessed!

ABOUT THE AUTHOR

Don is a loving husband, father, grandfather, pastor and friend who writes from the perspective of one who has been in pastoral ministry since 1968 with a keen interest and involvement in pastoral counselling for inner healing over more than 35 years.

With mounting pressure in the church to either condemn or condone different sexual lifestyles, Don bears witness to the fact that there is another and better way to minister the grace of God in a confused and broken world that brings ultimate glory to Jesus, our Wisdom, our Righteousness, our Sanctification, and our Redemption (I Cor. 1:30).